"It's Time"

Lois A. Hoshor

P O Box 547

Thornville, Ohio 43076-0547

E-Mail Address: soulseekers7@itilink.com

Phone: (740) 246-6272

Fax: (740) 246-6694

ISBN 0-9712935-0-3

Additional copies of this book available by mail.
Contact: Soul Seekers Evangelistic Association
P O Box 547
Thornville, Ohio 43076-0547

Printed in the USA by
BookMasters, Inc.
PO Box 2139
Mansfield, OH 44905
1-800-537-6727

It's Time

To every thing there is a season,
And a time to every purpose under the heaven:
A time to be born, and a time to die;
A time to plant, and a time to
Pluck up that which is planted;
A time to kill, and a time to heal;
A time to break down,
And a time to build up;
A time to weep, and a time to laugh;
A time to mourn, and a time to dance;
A time to cast away stones,
And a time to gather stones together;
A time to embrace,
And a time to refrain from embracing;
A time to get, and a time to lose;
A time to keep, and a time to cast away;
A time to rend, and a time to sew;
A time to keep silence,
And a time to speak;
A time to love, and a time to hate;
A time of war, and a time of peace.

Ecclesiastes 3:1~8

Endorsements

Lois Hoshor is my highly anointed friend from Ohio. I am always amazed at the energy she has at the altars and even more that that, the powerful words of revelation that God gives her for the starving Body of Christ. I have seen the hardest hearts fall to their knees at the word God gives through her. I can promise you she is one of the ones that "diligently seeks Him." Jesus Christ is truly Lord of her life. I am sure you will be blessed by this book and the healing touch it will have on your life. Lois is always welcome in the Upper Room in Alabama.

Bonnie Stinson
Founder of Women of Worth Ministries, Gadsden, Alabama

Having read Lois' book, the words that best describe my initial reaction were, "Timely and on Target." Everything that she wrote has been a continual work that the Lord has brought to my attention. Each chapter seemed to be something that I have preached on or been in conversation about in the last two years. Truly, "It's Time," is straight from the heart of the Lord and needs to be read by all believers searching and seeking for a word from the Lord. Lois has hit the nail on the head as to the condition of the body of Christ and its believers. She has truly heard God's voice and wrote as one lead of the Spirit of God. Anyone who has sought the face of God, and anyone who has been listening to the Spirit speak, knows that Lois is right on track with what the Lord is doing. Truly, this is a must read book. I will be recommending it to our entire congregation.

Michael Bullock
Pastor, Hands Of Faith Church, Zanesville, Ohio

Pastor Lois has a deep inner desire to better know the Lord, and she has a profound love and burden for all those who also seek to better know and serve the Lord. Thus, "It's Time" gives expression to her heart desire for visitation, in which lives will be changed and brought into a closer walk with the Lord. As she so clearly states in this book, it is only as we rise above our limitations, and turn aside from all of the activities that keep us from the Lord, that we will receive the visitation we so desire. The message in this book has been "wrought" out in the life and ministry of Pastor Lois through many experiences. She is well qualified to challenge us to go beyond our present spiritual experience. You will not only be greatly blessed, but you will be deeply challenged by this book. I highly recommend this book to you, for your prayerful reading.

Wade E. Taylor
Editor, The Banner
Founding President of Pinecrest Bible Institute, Salisbury, NY

This book wakes us up to the fact that time is short. For some, more than others. We have wasted a lot of time with frivolous preaching. We need to get our anointing back while it is still time. Time to put the wasted past behind us; time to put our hurts behind us. . . This is an anointed book which will wake us up and cause us to get blessed, shout, and come alive! Today is the day; yesterday is gone. Let's realize; This Is The Time.

Finley Hargett
Pastor, Calvary Road Community Church, Grove City, Ohio

Acknowledgements

I would like to thank everyone who so graciously helped with this project.

Sherry West, Mikki Holdeman, and Ginger Reed, for their time spent editing, spell checking, typesetting, and praying.

My husband, Bob, who understood when I closed myself off from the rest of the world to "hear" what the Lord was speaking to me.

To my church family at Firm Foundation Fellowship, for their prayers and support.

To the seed-sowers who believed in this project, not only with their words of encouragement and prayers, but also with their financial support.

But, most of all, I want to thank the Lord Jesus Christ for entrusting me with this, His Project.

To God Be The Glory!

Dedication

This book is dedicated to the memory of my earthly father, Merle Mason. Dad went home to be with the Lord in January 2000. He left behind a legacy of God's Love and the absolute that we will meet again soon.

To my mother, Ginny Mason, whose Faith, Love, and Hope of a brighter tomorrow has been a source of strength to all she has touched. One thing she taught me through the years was that, no matter how difficult things may seem to be, "This Too, Shall Pass."

Forward

There is a difference between a Bible commentary that shares one's opinion about the Bible and/or a particular passage thereof, and of a personal experience shared from the heart and soul. John, on the island of Patmos, was not sharing his **OPINION** about God; he was sharing his **EXPERIENCE** with God's power, glory, and revelation out of his **HEART** and **SOUL**. This book truly shares the **HEART** and **SOUL** of the author.

I have known Sister Lois for many years now. I have seen her from afar and from the inner circle as a friend. Lois is one in a million. We have ministered side~by~side, and I have seen first hand her sincere desire to please God in her life.

I feel that she has the insight of a prophet, and the faith of a child; furthermore, she is one of the most honest voices in the evangelistic world today.

This book is easy to read and is a true handbook of Christian spirituality. Lois touches on areas where few dare to tread. All of us that walk with the Lord have had experiences that were both beautiful and breathtaking, but few can honestly and accurately bring them to life with a pen.

The insight and awesome revelations contained in this book will truly challenge you in your walk with the Lord, and once you start reading it you will not want to put it down.

This is the TIME for the Church to walk in its fullness, and I believe that this book is one more powerful glimpse of God's glory. I thank God for the insight and guidance given, and the true mark of leadership seen in this book.

When all is said and done, and this book is closed, you will say, **"SHE MADE A DIFFERENCE!"**

Pastor Keith D. Clary
New Breath Assembly of God
Washington C.H., Ohio

Table of Contents

All Scripture references are from the King James
Version of the Holy Bible unless otherwise noted.

"It's Time"

INTRODUCTION

As the Lord began to lay upon my heart the writing of this book, I heard Him speak to my spirit, "It's Time." I had heard this many times throughout the years in reference to various periods in my life, so my immediate thought was, "time for **what?**" Well, as usual, I put off the actual getting in the presence of the Lord to get my instructions. It has been my character to put off the things of the Lord that I know will bring with it more responsibility, more time, more money, and more *dying to self!* For some reason, we tend to think that we have to do whatever gets done. The Lord therefore, has impressed on me the importance of **knowing** that all He requires of us is **obedience** and **trust** in Him! As we continue to learn and grow in Him, we will see His hand working in our behalf. As we practice **His presence** in our life, we will then be moved from just "seeing His hand" to "seeing His face." Psalm 103:7 says: *"He made known his ways unto Moses, his acts unto the children of Israel."* I have determined in my heart to "know His ways." The only way this is going to happen is by coming into His presence, heeding to His voice, and obeying the words of instruction that are given to us. After I received the nudging of the Holy Spirit to begin this work, I sought confirmation as to the direction I should go. I spoke with a good friend, Max Stinson, from Gadsden, Alabama, and he said he had a word for me from the Lord. He then proceeded to tell me that it was time to start on my next book. He had a vision of this book with that same title and a picture of an hourglass on the front cover. I was astounded because that was the exact same dream I had had several weeks before. I didn't tell anyone what I felt the Lord was saying. Several weeks passed and my daughter, Ginger, paged me while I was on the road. I called home to hear her say to me that she felt it was **really time** for me to begin my next book. She felt the Lord had given her some insight as to the content and wanted to encourage me to **heed to the voice of the Lord!!!** I shared with my husband, Bob, the entire account of my conversation with Ginger. He then said to me, "I can't believe this. Last night I was up in the middle of the night, and the thought just came to me, "It's time for Lois to start another book!" Well, I guess I am one of God's slow children, but I am finally getting the message. **"It's Time!**

As I shared with our home fellowship group, they too, had a witness that God is getting ready to release a mighty outpouring of His Spirit upon the earth. We **must** get ready . . . **Now** is the time! But, **time for what???**

If you open your heart and ask the Lord to give you ears to hear what the Spirit is saying to the church, you will hear His Voice speak to you through the pages that follow. Get ready . . .

Chapter 1

The Perfect Time

What is time? I looked in the dictionary and was amazed to find half a page explaining what time is. Just a few of the explanations are as follows:

1. Indefinite, unlimited duration in which things are considered as happening in the past, present, or future; every moment there has ever been or ever will be.
2. The period between two events or during which something exists, happens, or acts.
3. A period characterized by a prevailing condition or specific experience.
4. The point at which something has happened, is happening, or will happen.
5. The usual, natural, traditional, or appointed moment for something to begin.

Now that is just a few of man's explanations for time. What does God say about time?

In Ecclesiastes 3:1~8, the Lord tells us this:

"To every thing there is a season, and a time to every purpose under the heaven: A time to be born, and a time to die; a time to plant, and a time to pluck up that which is planted; A time to kill, and a time to heal; a time to break down, and a time to build up; A time to weep, and a time to laugh; a time to mourn, and a time to dance; A time to cast away stones, and a time to gather stones together; a time to embrace, and a time to refrain from embracing; A time to get, and a time to lose; a time to keep, and a time to cast away; A time to rend, and a time to sew; a time to keep silence, and a time to speak; a time to love, and a time to hate; a time of war, and a time of peace."

The Lord then goes on to say in verse 11(a) that He has made everything beautiful in His Time. Well, I would say that we may have found a key to time! It must be God's Time for it to bring forth the beauty, the fulfillment, the peace, and the purpose of God's plan in our life. The Apostle Paul wrote to the church at Ephesis the following:

This is my life work: helping people understand and respond to this Message. It came as a sheer gift to me, a real surprise, God handling all the details. When it came to presenting the Message to people who had no background in God's way, I was the least qualified of any of the available Christians. God saw to it that I was equipped, but you can be sure that it had nothing to do with my natural abilities. And so here I am, preaching and writing about things that are way over my head, the inexhaustible riches and generosity of Christ. My task is to bring out in the open and make plain what God, who created all this in the first place, has been doing in secret and behind the scenes all along. Through Christians like yourselves gathered in churches, this extraordinary plan of God is becoming known and talked about even among the angels!" (Ephesians 3:7~11 The Message Bible)

Paul knew that he was in God's perfect timing. He knew that it was not with his own giftings and talents that this would be accomplished, but through the mighty power of the Lord working through him. Can you relate to the statement that Paul made when he said that he was writing about things that were way over his head? I know I sure can! How did he say this message of the mysteries of God would get out to the world? Through "Christians like yourselves, gathered in churches" around the world. That's Us!!

I believe that the Church of Jesus Christ has now entered into a time of "Last Day Anointing - Last Day Power - Last Day Purpose - and Last Day Revelation" like the world has never seen.

The point the Lord wants to make to us is, we are part of this plan! It's Time for the church to rise up in the power of His might! It's Time for His children to stand up and be counted. It's Time for the Revelation of the Power of the Anointing of God to be released to the world. Isaiah 40:5 says: "And the glory of the Lord shall be revealed, and all flesh shall see it together: for the mouth of the Lord hath spoken it." Do you have to believe it for it to happen? No . . . Do you even have to get in on it for it to happen? No . . . But what if it really isn't the time for this to take place? It doesn't matter who you are, how young or old, how rich or poor you may be, **your** time is running out! **You** are closer to Eternity today than you have **ever** been in your life! We **must** get the understanding - **TIME IS RUNNING OUT** - so whatever you plan to do, **"It's Time."**

The Lord spoke a Prophetic Word several months ago and in that Word He told us that He was going to have a people who would walk with Him in honesty, integrity, and purity of heart. He also said that He **would** have a people that had "clean hands and a pure heart." He said He was going to "Baptize us anew in a Baptism of His Love."

Again I want to go to Paul's writings, this time to the church at Rome. In Romans 13:10~14 we are given a mighty word of instruction as to the element of God's Love, but also of the importance of **time**.

"Love worketh no ill to his neighbor: therefore love is the fulfilling of the law. And that, knowing the time, that now it is high time to awake out of sleep: for now is our salvation nearer than when we believed. The night is far spent, the day is at hand: let us therefore cast off the works of darkness, and let us put on the armor of light. Let us walk honestly, as in the day; not in rioting and drunkenness, not in chambering and wantonness, not in strife and envying. But put ye on the Lord Jesus Christ, and make not provision for the flesh, to fulfill the lusts thereof."

Not only does Paul let us know that it's time, but that it's **high time** to put on the Lord Jesus Christ. Who does that? **We do!**

If you are not convinced that it is time for **you** to become all that the Lord has created you to be, then the remainder of this book will **not** speak to you. But, if you **know** you are a part of this last day great outpouring of His Spirit, then **read on**. For **Truly, The Best Is Yet To Come . . .**

Chapter 2

God's Dimensions Of Relationships

Have you ever thought that the Lord seems to love some people more than He does others? Have you ever wondered why some seem to hear so clearly the voice of the Lord and many others don't have a clue as to the workings of the Spirit? They are Christians, yet they do not have that "experiential testimony" that will transform their life. Is it just that God has favorites and pours out more of His blessings to certain "chosen vessels"? Well, I want you to know something right now! It is **not** degrees of Love, but the Dimension of the Relationship that determines what and how much we receive from the Lord. Who decides that? **We do**.

I am going to outline several dimensions of relationships with the Lord that are spelled out in the Word. I want you to get downright honest with yourself and with the Lord and determine to find out where **you** stand in this plan of God. First of all, we need to realize that the Lord's desire from the very beginning was that "all" the world would be saved.

1. God's Plan: The World

John 3:17 says: *"For God sent not His Son into the world to condemn the world; but that the world through Him, might be saved."*

Now we all realize that the entire world is not, nor will be, saved. But, that fact does not alter the heart of God for the world to come to Him. So, we have a world of people that are lost and dying without the love of Christ in their hearts. It is there for them, but they refuse to receive that free gift from God. There is absolutely **nothing** God can do with a people that refuse His love. Their dimension of relationship is **zero**!!

2. God's Chosen: The Nation of Israel

Psalm 106:4,5 says: *"Remember me, O Lord with the favour that thou bearest unto thy people: O visit me with thy salvation. That I may see the good of thy chosen, that I may rejoice in the gladness of thy nation, that I may glory with thine inheritance."*

We all know that the nation of Israel was God's chosen people. A covenant was made with Abraham, and a promise given that through his seed all the world would be blessed. We can read of this account in Genesis 12:1~3.

> *Now the Lord had said unto Abram, Get thee out of thy country, and from thy kindred, and from thy father's house, unto a land that I will show thee: And I will make of thee a great nation, and I will bless thee, and make thy name great; and thou shalt be a blessing: And I will bless them that bless, and curse them that curseth thee: and in thee shall all families of the earth be blessed.*

We know that the Lord did bless Abraham and Sarah with a son they named Isaac; who in turn had a son they called Jacob, whose name was later changed to Israel. This son, Jacob, had twelve sons who became known as the tribes of Israel. We can follow the lineage from Abraham to David to Jesus that is recorded in Matthew, chapter one, and see how the original promise that was given to Abraham was fulfilled. We can also read in Galatians 3:29 the continuance of this promise to the world. *"And if ye be Christ's, then are ye Abraham's seed, and heirs according to the promise."*

We therefore can know, through the Word of God, that He had a plan for His chosen people.

3. The Watchers & the Getters: or the Multitudes

Matthew 4:23~25 talks about this group of people. *"And Jesus went about all of Galilee, teaching in their synagogues, and preaching the gospel of the kingdom, and healing all manner of sickness and all manner of disease among the people. And his fame went throughout all Syria: and they brought unto him all sick people that were taken with divers diseases and torments, and those which were possessed with devils, and those which were lunatic, and those that had palsy; and he healed them. And there followed him great multitudes of people, from Galilee, and from Decapolis, and from Jerusalem, and from Judea, and from beyond Jordan."* These watchers and getters became followers of the Lord for one reason. To **get something from Him**.

26

There is a group of people in the church today that are still just watchers and getters. What can you **do** for **me?** What will I get out of this relationship? This group of people take the Name of Jesus, but many times they take His Name in vain. They want to be known as a Christian, a member of the church, a follower of the Lord, but they don't want to put forth any effort to accomplish anything. They want the preacher to **catch** the fish, **clean** the fish, **cook** the fish, and then call them to dinner. It is just a "gimme, gimme, gimme," world they live in. Gimme this and gimme that, and I don't want to have to **do** anything to get it! Instead of "Lord, what can you do for me?"; the Lord is raising up a people that are going to say: "Lord, what can I do for you?"

Then along came:

4. The Followers

Luke 10:1 says: *"After these things, the Lord appointed other seventy also, and sent them two and two before his face into every city and place, whither he himself would come."* These seventy were sent out by the Lord into every city where he intended to go and minister to the people. What an honor to be a part of the sent ones. Something we need to realize

27

with this group of disciples. They were sent forth with power and authority over all the power of the enemy. But, they were not given the authority over the government of the church in the realm of the natural. This is where the leaders of the present day church miss the Lord. Many times, in order to please man, they delegate authority in the natural realm to people that are not equipped to oversee the leadership of the church. This brings schism in the body if it is not corrected the proper way. We will talk about this in more depth in a later chapter.

5. The Twelve

The Lord called twelve disciples to be "workers in the field" for him. The were a motley crew, to say the least! We have Simon Peter, and his brother Andrew, who were smelly fishermen. We then have James and John, who were also in the family business of fishing. Then there is Bartholomew; Philip; Thomas, the doubter; Matthew, the tax collector; James; Thaddaeus; Simon, the Canaanite; and Judas, the betrayer. They could not have been a very promising group of leaders, but the Lord saw beyond the natural, into the realm of the spirit, and into the plan and purpose of God.

Matthew 10:1 says: *"And when he had called unto him his twelve disciples, he gave unto them power against unclean spirits, to cast them out, and to heal all manner of sickness and all manner of disease."* The Lord gave them power over all the power of the enemy! What a chosen realm of the circle to be in. We then find after the day of Pentecost, that they were given the authority of Apostleship to establish the church. However, very few were permitted to enter into yet another realm.

6. The Circle of Three; or The Inner Circle

In Matthew 17:1~3, we can read a little about this Inner Circle. *"And after six days Jesus taketh Peter, James, and John his brother, and bringeth them up into a high mountain apart, And was transfigured before them: and his face did shine as the sun, and his raiment was white as the light. And, behold, there appeared unto them Moses and Elijah talking with him."* We can look throughout the Word of God and see where Jesus took with him just Peter, James, and John. Have you ever wondered what the other disciples must have thought? With all of the envy and jealousy that is in the Body of Christ today, I have to wonder what was said amongst the other disciples.

29

These three were at the Transfiguration; they were at Gethsemane; they were taken to the house of Jairus, to see his daughter raised from the dead; they were that **Inner Circle**. The **Chosen of God**. Did the Lord love them more? It was not a matter of the degree of Love, but the degree of **Relationship**! I believe they were friends of the Lord. In John 15:15, the Lord says: *"Henceforth, I call you not servants; for the servant knoweth not what his Lord doeth: but I have called you friends; for all things that I have heard of my Father I have made known unto you."* All of the twelve were not privy to everything that the Lord shared; but these three of that Inner Circle were. Through the years, we have had some awesome experiences that everyone around us just did not have. Many times that can cause some people to think they just are not as spiritual as others. Many times it can cause spiritual jealousy and division, instead of a hunger stirring in their spirit, like the Lord wants it to. There are times that spiritual experiences can be used by the enemy to cause pride and arrogance to rise up within a soul. Thus, we must be constantly on guard against this if we are walking in a realm of spiritual experience that is not considered the "norm" for the church. We

30

have seen the cloud of glory fill the room; we have seen the gold dust fall; we have experienced the fragrance of the Lord's presence; we have heard the voice of many waters that stirred us to our very bones. I have seen the angels with my natural eyes and heard them raise their voice in praise to the King of Glory. Many times, the oil of the Lord has been manifested in our midst. Does this mean He loves us more (those of us that get to experience these manifestations)? No! It is NOT degrees of love, but the degree of relationship. You can read about the ministers of old that had great moves of the power of God or great manifestations of His presence in their lives, and you will find that they spent a **lot** of time in His presence; a lot of time in prayer; a lot of time in praise; and a lot of time fasting . . . **They had a greater degree of relationship!** Oh, to be called a friend of the Lord! Finally, we have one more realm of relationship.

7. One With The Father

We can see in Matthew 26:6~46, how the Lord told the three of the "Inner Circle" to wait while he went to that place of solitude; that place of being alone with the Father. The Lord knew what it meant to have that one-on-one relationship with God. He knew the importance of experiencing the intimacy that can come only from time alone with Father God. We can see throughout the Word of God those that entered into that one-on-one intimate relationship with the Lord. They have names like; Moses, Enoch, Philip, John (on the isle of Patmos), Deborah, Esther, and the Marys'. The Lord wants a people that will be willing to pay the price to go from being just part of the world, to being part of that inner circle, or that "called out from amongst them" group. We can not experience that unless we have our Gethsemane. We must get into an intimate relationship with the Lord.

Many times, as ministers of the Gospel, we tend to miss the leading of the Lord by giving out that "Inner Circle Revelation" to the multitudes. This must stop! With all our getting, the Lord is wanting us to get **understanding**. So many times, prophetic words are spoken out of season to the wrong people and the message of the Lord is missed. We must be willing to have that single eye of the dove that is spoken of in the Song of Solomon; seeing only the Lord and His plan for our life. That will require total commitment!

Psalm 42:7 says: *"Deep calleth unto deep at the noise of thy waterspouts: all thy waves and thy billows are gone over me."*

The Lord is going to have a people that will allow the **deep** to call unto the **deep**. Having heard what the cost is going to be, are you still willing to go forth with the plan of the Lord for your life?

Chapter Three

The Hand Of God

The Hand of the Lord is working in the world today through what the church calls the five-fold offices of apostle, prophet, evangelist, pastor, and teacher. This can be found in Ephesians 4:11,12. *"And he gave some, apostles; and some, prophets; and some, evangelists; and some, pastors and teachers; For the perfecting of the saints, for the work of the ministry, for the edifying of the body of Christ."*

How long is He going to do this? *"Till we all come in the unity of the faith, and of the knowledge of the Son of God, unto a perfect man, unto the measure of the stature of the fulness of Christ . . . ."*

In today's church, we can easily find evangelists, pastors, or teachers. But, where are the apostles and prophets? I want us to look at our own hand and envision the various parts of the hand of God.

1. The Thumb

This is a type and shadow of the office of apostle. The thumb works well with every other finger on the hand. The job of the apostle is to **Govern**. An apostle will help establish new works, get the house in order, help set up the God ordained authority, or bring correction and chastisement to "out of order" leadership if necessary.

Now we can begin to understand the reason why the church is being so lax in recognizing the apostlic office.

2. The First Finger

This finger represents the prophet. The purpose of the prophet is to **Guide**. This is the "pointer" finger. A **true prophet** will guide and direct under the unction of the Holy Ghost. He will truly hear from the Lord and therefore, give Godly direction. A prophet is not out to make a name for himself or to build a big ministry. Many times a prophet will not even make himself known to anyone other than the church leadership, until the time is right for him to speak forth the word of the Lord. A prophet, in the natural realm, can be very intimidating and seems to appear arrogant. Look at the prophets in the Word like Elijah; Elisha; or the prophetess, Deborah. If the leadership in the church is not assured of their postition in Christ, then the office of prophet will be rejected by them. They will be threatened by the very presence of a true prophet of God. Now you understand why there are not more prophets acknowledged by the "established church."

It is **not** the fact that there are no apostles or prophets in the world today, they just are not being accepted of the brethren!

That is about to change, because It's Time.

3. The Index Finger

This represents the evangelist. This finger extends out past the rest. It reaches further to touch what other fingers on their own may not reach. The evangelist's job is to **Gather**. An anointed evangelist will bring in a crowd that the pastor cannot seem to reach. He will search out the hearts of men and women and cause them to feel they have been personally touched by the hand of God. He will encourage, edify, build up, and minister new life in a way the rest of the hand is unable to do. There are many great evangelists on the mission field. They may never have a "big" name, or be well-known in religious circles, but they are great evangelists is the heavenlies.

4. The Ring Finger

It has been said that this is the only finger that has a direct line to the heart. We place our wedding ring on this finger. It denotes a special kind of love. That is why this represents the pastor. The pastor has a special kind of love for his flock. His call and purpose; to **Guard**. He is like the shepherd that watches over the sheep to protect them from the spritual "wolves" and to see to it that they are fed, watered, and properly nourished. A person that tries to pastor without a pastor's heart will end up with a bunch of malnourished and discontented sheep. They will be spiritually famished and dry. A pastor must love in a way like no other. A "called by God" pastor will learn how to protect his sheep without manipulating and controlling them. The heart of God will be seen in his life and in his actions.

5. The Little Finger

Also known as the "pinky," this is the finger you use to dig and probe and represents the teacher. The purpose of the teacher is to **Ground**. We **must** be grounded in the Word of God. We **must** discern the truth of God's Word. We **must** be in a constant mode of learning and growing in the power of His might. How can this happen if there are no God ordained teachers? I want you to notice something in this passage of scripture. In verse 11 it says: *"And he gave some, apostles; and some, prophets; and some, evangelists; and some, pastors and teachers. . . . "* He gave **some** of each one **except** teachers. I do not believe that this means that the office of pastor and teacher are one and the same. I believe that the Lord wants us to realize that we are **all called and anointed** for service in His body. I believe the Lord is saying to us, "if you are not an apostle; if you are not a prophet; if you are not an evangelist; if you are not a pastor; **then** you can know you are called to teach others what you have learned and received from the rest of the hand of God.

Why do I believe that? Because the Lord went on to tell us in verse 12 the purpose of the hand of God working in the church. *". . . For the perfecting of the saints* (that's us), *for the work of the ministry* (for what purpose?), *for the edifying* (or building up) *of the body of Christ."* For this to

38

happen, it is going to take **all** of the hand of God doing their part . . . and that includes the "little finger." For this to happen, the church is going to have to get in that place where they **know** who they are in Christ and who He is in them! The Lord is shouting from the heavens: **IT'S TIME.** How can this happen? What do we need to do to get into that place of complete obedience? We must realize, first of all, that we can't get there from here!

Chapter 4

We Just Can't Get There From Here

Genesis 12:1~3, *"Now the Lord had said unto Abram, Get thee out of thy country, and from thy kindred, and from thy father's house; unto a land that I will show thee: And I will make of thee a great nation, and I will bless thee, and make thy name great; and thou shalt be a blessing: And I will bless them that bless thee, and curse him that curseth thee: and in thee shall all families of the earth be blessed."* The very next verse says: *"So Abram departed, as the Lord had spoken unto him; and Lot went with him . . ."* (Genesis 12:4a). What about "get out of thy country and from thy kindred" did he **not** understand?

The very first thing Abram did was walk in a place of "partial obedience." We all know what happened because Lot went along! The Lord wants His people to start understanding the consequences of "partial obedience" to the voice of God.

In Acts 7:1~3 we have the story of Stephen being taken before the high priest to give account of the reason behind the "signs and wonders" that are being done everywhere he goes. Now Stephen was appointed a "deacon" in the church, along with five other men, to see to it that the widows were receiving proper care. **Why is he performing miracles?** He is supposed to be working in the soup kitchen!

Total obedience to the call of God in our life, whether it is being a doctor; lawyer; store or factory worker; or housewife and mother, will produce the miracles of God! Miracles are made up of two parts; impossible circumstances and total obedience!

Now, back to Stephen. He starts off with: *". . . The God of glory appeared unto our father Abraham, when he was in Mesopotamia, before he dwelt in Haran, And said unto him, Get thee out of thy country, and from thy kindred, and come into the land which I shall show thee."* (Acts 7:2,3) Stephen then continues with an account of the process that led to them being where they were. He tells about the birth of the twelve sons (tribes) of Abraham, through his son, Isaac; through his son, Jacob. He tells of the jealousy of Joseph's brothers, and about his being sold into slavery. He goes on to tell them that every word that God spoke to Abraham came to pass. Just as God had said, once the king rose to power that did not know Joseph, he took God's people captive as slaves in the land of Egypt for 400 years.

Still, the promises of God are "yea and amen." He had a deliverer in the making and Moses was born. But, Moses tried to do it his way and spent forty years on the backside of the desert getting prepared.

Stephen concludes his oracle with these words: *"Ye stiffnecked and uncircumcised in heart and ears, ye do always resist the Holy Ghost: as your fathers did, so do ye."* (Acts 7:51) Well, needless to say, Stephen was stoned to death. But look at this account in Acts 7:54~60:

> *When they heard these things, they were cut to the heart, and they gnashed on him with their teeth. But he, being full of the Holy Ghost, looked up steadfastly into heaven, and saw the glory of God, and Jesus standing on the right hand of God, And said, Behold, I see the heavens opened, and the Son of man standing on the right hand of God. Then they cried out with a loud voice, and stopped their*

ears, ran upon him with one accord, And cast him out of the city, and stoned him: and the witnesses laid down their clothes at a young man's feet, whose name was Saul. And they stoned Stephen, calling upon God, and saying, Lord Jesus, receive my spirit. And he kneeled down, and cried with a loud voice, Lord, lay not this sin to their charge. And when he had said this, he fell asleep.

Can we even begin to comprehend the power of the Lord that was being manifested upon Stephen at this time? Hebrews 1:3 says: *"Who being the brightness of his glory, and the express image of his person, and upholding all things by the word of his power, when he had by himself purged our sins, sat down on the right hand of the Majesty on high."* But Stephen saw the Lord **standing**. I can tell you, when you see the Lord **stand up** in your behalf, **something** is about to happen!

What a price that was paid from the time of the promise of God that was given to Abraham, to the time of the fulfillment of that promise. We all want the promises of God to be fulfilled in our own life; but, we want the easy road to success. I have to tell you this: **You just can't get there from where you are**. There is a "highway of Holiness" that we must walk on to get to the fulfillment of the promises of God in our life. Hebrews 11:8~10 lets us know the extent of that. *"By faith Abraham, when he was called to go out into a place which he should after receive for an inheritance, obeyed; and he went out, not knowing whither he went. By faith he sojourned in the land of promise, as in a strange country, dwelling in tabernacles with Isaac and Jacob, the heirs with him of the same promise: For he looked for a city which hath foundations, whose builder and maker is God."*

What is the answer to getting the promises of God? Looking beyond your present circumstances and knowing you really can't get there from here. You must move on in Him. You must be willing to go to that place, not knowing where it leads; but, putting your faith and trust in God to get you there. Does your faith move mountains, or do your mountains move your faith? You will never be able to stand on the promises if you are just sitting on the premises. We must move on in Him! Has anyone besides me ever wondered, "How can I get that kind of faith that will move mountains and lift me higher in the realm of the spirit? Lord, I believe with every thing in me; or, do I? How can I walk in "true faith?"

To get to the place the Lord has destined for us to go, something has to change. None of us can go higher in the things of the Lord, and stay where we are. The one thing that people do not want to embrace in their lives is change. We are creatures of habit. We **like** knowing what is going to happen in our daily routine. We **like** knowing from where our paycheck is going to come, and knowing exactly how much it is going to be. We want to know our friends and church family are dependable and will be there anytime we need them.

Most of us even like to have the furniture in our homes to remain in the same place (especially the men!). But change is a "necessary evil," if you will, for growth to be experienced. We want to walk in **true faith**. Does that mean there can be a faith that is **not** true faith?

Chapter 5

Unfeigned Faith

"Now the end of the commandment is charity out of a pure heart, and of a good conscience, and of faith unfeigned." (I Timothy 1:5) The word unfeigned means, sincere or without hypocrisy. Our faith must be sincere and without hypocrisy for it to be **true** faith. This word tells me that if there is unfeigned faith (or the real thing); then, there is a definite possibility that a **false** faith can exist.

In II Timothy 1:5~7, we have an interesting scenario. Paul is talking through this letter to his spiritual son, Timothy. He says: "When I call to remembrance the unfeigned faith that is in thee, which dwelt first in thy grandmother Lois, and thy mother Eunice; and I am persuaded that in thee also. Wherefore I put thee in remembrance that thou stir up the gift of God, which is in thee by the putting on of my hands. For God hath not given us the spirit of fear; but of power, and of love, and of a sound mind."

Paul, in essence, is saying to Timothy: "I know that you have genuine faith because I see it not only in your grandmother, but in your mother also. They in turn have transferred this down the generations and you now have that same kind of faith."

He has the boldness to go on and say that Timothy had spiritual gifts in him that were a result of Paul laying hands on him to receive. He not only reminds him of that, he also lets him know that it is not God's plan for him to be fearful in anything. The Lord has given him the spirit of power, love, and a sound mind. You can know in your "knower" that the Lord has gifted you with His mighty power!

But doesn't that sound presumptuous and arrogant? Not at all! That merely sounds like you know who you are in Christ and who He is in you. That even looks like unfeigned faith! The word of God has promised us so much more than we are walking in, and the Lord is saying: "It's Time." Time to stand up in faith believing that every promise in the book is mine!

There is a very important fact that we must get into our spirit if we are going to walk in the promises of God's Word with health, wealth, wisdom, and power. We do not receive according to God's power and ability; we receive according to our faith. The Lord has given us example after example of this truth throughout His Word. We must hear with our spirit what the Lord is speaking to us!

In Matthew 9, we have the story of the woman that touched the hem of His garment. In verse 22, the Lord says: *". . . Daughter, be of good comfort; thy faith hath made thee whole."* The woman was made whole that very hour. Shortly after, two blind men come up to Jesus and ask him to give them their sight. The Lord asked them if they really believed He could do this; they answered and said they did. The Lord then touched their eyes and said: *"According to your faith be it unto you."*

We must get the understanding that faith varies from area to area. Faith for healing comes from hearing about healing. Faith for prosperity comes from hearing about the blessing of God through prosperity. Faith must be developed in the area needed! How can I tell if what I have is real faith?

1. Real Faith comes from receiving a real word from the Lord. It must be Rhema! What God has spoken to your spirit personally. You can **not** get healed or delivered by **my** Rhema word. It has to be **your** Rhema word. We have two words for "word" in the Bible. One is logos, which means the written word; the other is Rhema, which means living word.

Jesus said in John 6:63b: *". . . the words that I speak unto you, they are spirit, and they are life."* (Emphasis mine) Therefore, we must hear Him speak to us personally. This is a personal thing. We are all familiar with the Scripture in Hebrew 11:1 that says: *"Now faith is the substance of things hoped for, the evidence of things not seen."* (Emphasis mine) What kind of faith is Jesus talking about? **Now faith!** The word **now**, is an adjective not a conjunction. It is describing what kind of faith we are to have.

2. Faith is the foundation or the basis for what is expected. **Hope!** We have on our hands a generation of "hopeless" people. The young people are without hope of a brighter tomorrow. There are so many children in this country of America that are finding themselves in the "system" of foster care. They are without hope. Proverbs 13:12 says: *"Hope deferred maketh the heart sick: but when the desire cometh, it is a tree of life."* Listen to how the Message

Bible says it: *"Unrelenting disappointment leaves you heartsick, but a sudden good break can turn life around."*

We need to offer these people, including the young people, a ray of hope for their tomorrows. The only true hope is in Jesus Christ. Once they get this hope, then they will be able to experience what faith, true faith, is all about. Remember, faith is the foundation or the true basis for what is expected. That "sudden good break" of which the Message Bible speaks.

I know of a situation where a child was adopted out of the foster care system. His biological parents did not want him and made that very clear. After being in this home for several years as an adopted son, the adoptive parents gave him back to the system. This child was twice rejected by parents he thought he could count on to love him and take care of him. Do you realize how difficult it will be to ever convince this child that he has a Heavenly Father that loves him and cares for his every need? Only the power of God's Love will ever set him free from the deep-seated roots of rejection and disappointment. This is only one of thousands of examples that I could share with you. True faith

50

must be shown to that hopeless generation or they will never be saved. Are you walking in unfeigned faith?

3. If we believe something we are convinced. I know that Jesus loves me and will never leave me or forsake me, regardless of what may be going on in my present life or situations. I have that true faith in my spirit and there is nothing that can take that away from me! I, like Timothy, had this handed down to me from my great-grandparents, to my grandparents, to my parents. I, in turn, have been able to hand it down to my children and grandchildren. **What an awesome blessing from the Lord.**

You may not have had this come down your family tree, but you can hand it on down to your children and grandchildren if you are now walking in true faith. You have to have the "I know so" in your spirit; that "I know, that I know, that I know." Remember, we are talking about true faith that will change your life!

4. God does not respond according to His ability, but according to our faith! Most of us know God can do anything. But, for what do we really believe? **Faith is not need! Faith is not desire! Faith is not want!**

I heard a preacher give an example of "false faith" one time that really spoke to my heart. I was raised Pentecostal, so I have seen, first hand, many examples of false faith.

This minister told the story of his car battery being dead and his car would not start. A "faith" bible school student asked him why he didn't just "speak" to the battery to be charged and start the car. Well, the truth of the matter was that the battery was old and needed replaced. He had the faith to believe for the money to buy a new battery, but he did not have the faith to speak new life into the old one.

We must learn to walk in the level of faith where we are, (use what we have) so God can bring the increase. Many times we are guilty of twisting the scripture that says: ". . . and calleth those things which be not as though they were" (Romans 4:17b); and we try to speak those things that **are** as though they **were not**. We must rightfully divide the Word of Truth. The Lord was speaking in reference to Abraham being called the father of many nations;

and it is referring to God being the one that calls things that are not as though they were.

When we try to use this Scripture and call it faith, many times it brings disappointment and despair. We hear a preacher excited in the Word speak this in the wrong way; then we try it. When it doesn't work, what happens in our life? We think faith doesn't work; but true, unfeigned faith **always works**. Remember, we do not receive according to God's ability, but according to our faith!

If your faith level is not where it needs to be to receive the promises of God in your life, there is an answer. Faith is **more** than just confession. We need to make positive confessions, but there is more to it than that. Unfeigned faith cannot be separated from being led by the Spirit of God. Remember John 6:63: *"It is the spirit that quickeneth; the flesh profiteth nothing: the words that I speak unto you, they are spirit, and they are life."* You notice that Jesus did not say "all the words that I have spoken." He said, "the words that I speak **unto you** they are spirit and they are life" or living Rhema words!

Walking in faith is not ignoring circumstances. That is the kind of thing that makes Spirit-filled Christians look ignorant. There are times we may have to look foolish for Christ's sake, but denying the facts is not the way to do it. If you are in pain, do **not** say that you are not. If you have bills that need to be paid, do **not** say that you are debt free. You can declare the Lord is going to bring you into that place of being free from pain or debt, but do **not** try to speak those things that **are** as though they **were not**.

Walking in faith is not ignoring the facts or circumstances of life. That is fake faith! False confession is not true faith. If you want to know how you can get and release into your life that true, unfeigned faith the Word of God talks about, continue reading!

Chapter 6

Releasing Your Faith

Before we can release our faith, we have to have it. How can we get faith? How can we get those that are without hope to believe? There is only one way! Romans 10:14~17 has the answer.

How then shall they call on him in whom they have not believed? and how shall they believe in him of whom they have not heard? and how shall they hear without a preacher? And how shall they preach, except they be sent? as it is written, How beautiful are the feet of them that preach the gospel of peace, and bring glad tidings of good things! But they have not all obeyed the gospel. For Isaiah saith, Lord, who hath believed our report? So then faith cometh by hearing and hearing by the word of God.

There is no other way! Faith comes by hearing, and hearing by the word of God! You must hear the word of God in order to get faith. Now, look at Romans 4:18~21. Again, this is talking about Abraham believing God will make him the father of nations. *"Who against hope believed in hope, that he might become the father of many nations, according to that which was spoken, So shall thy seed be. And being not weak in faith, he considered not his own body now dead, when he was about an hundred years old, neither yet the deadness of Sarah's womb: He staggered not at the promise of God through unbelief; but was strong in faith, giving glory to God; And being fully persuaded that, what he had promised, he was able also to perform."*

Abraham did not say he was young and full of vigor; he did not say that Sarah was at the perfect age to conceive; neither did he say, "I hope this really happens." The Word says, he was "fully persuaded" that what the Lord had said He would do, He would do! That is why he was later willing and able to offer Isaac on the altar of sacrifice, because he knew the promises of God are "yea and amen."

The promised seed was through his son, Isaac, not Ishmael. The Lord spoke an awesome revelation to me several years ago that has changed my life. He said **fact** and **truth** are not always the same thing. The fact can be you are rightfully diagnosed with an illness; but, the truth says, by His stripes, you are healed. Fact can be that you are thousands of dollars in debt; but, truth says, my God shall supply all my needs according to His riches in glory by Christ Jesus. The fact may very well be that you really do not have anything to give; but, the truth says, give and it shall be given unto you; pressed down, shaken together, and running over.

Jesus tells us in John 14:6, *". . . I am the way, the truth, and the life: no man cometh unto the Father, but by me."* In the beginning was the Word; and the Word became flesh and dwelt among men.

Remember, false confession is not faith! Take a small step of faith, get what you are believing for, and be encouraged to grow to another level of faith. The Lord uses people to give encouragement to us to believe for more from the Lord through their testimonies.

So many times I have heard a word of testimony from someone's life in regard to healing or financial miracles that stirred my faith to go higher in Him. But I had to first hear the Lord speak to my heart. I could not get there by riding in someone else's faith mobile.

I have a friend that has gone through one physical problem after another. She was in a place of total discouragement when she listened to the Word of God that talked about the promises of healing and blessing for His children. Her faith level rose to a new place, and she made a decision to just **do** something that she had not been able to do for a long time. She called and asked me to pray that she would have enough energy to clean her bathroom! Now, I must tell you, that would not have been my request, but she really enjoyed being able to clean her bathroom. She called the next day to let me know that God had honored her faith, and she cleaned her bathroom for the first time in nine months. This new level of faith worked in her a renewed hope for better things to come.

Now faith, is the substance of things hoped for, the evidence of things to come. See how it works? You need faith for the vision God has given you! Not someone else, but you!!

You must feed your faith and feed your vision. How can you feed your faith? **With the Word of God.**

Matthew 17:20 says: *". . . I say unto you, If ye have faith as a grain of mustard seed, ye shall say unto this mountain, Remove hence to yonder place; and it shall remove; and nothing shall be impossible unto you."* The Lord said it does not take great big faith to do something. It only has to be the size of a grain of mustard seed. A mustard seed, when planted, grows into a tree. You plant your faith for it to grow.

Understand also, that you have to **do** something! You shall **say** unto the mountain! Speak the power of the Word of God to the circumstances in your life. We are so busy trying to figure out how to make things happen that we miss the obvious. Stop speaking **words**, and start speaking **The Word**. Feed your faith; feed your vision!

This is more than "name it, claim it!" This is the power of the Word of God being released into your spirit.

In Mark 9:23, *"Jesus said unto him, If thou canst believe, all things are possible to him that believeth."* Kathryn Kulman used to stand on the platform with the anointing of God surrounding her. She would raise her hands toward heaven and say, "only believe." She would then reiterate the fact that whatever happened was the power of God, through

Jesus Christ, by the Holy Ghost. Only believe; all things are possible if we only believe! What a powerful word. We make it so difficult when Jesus made it so simple. **Only believe!**

How can we get this kind of faith? I tell people everywhere I go; put it in, put it in, put it in. . . and the Lord will bring it forth with His power and anointing. If we do our part, I can guarantee He will do His part. Remember, faith comes by hearing, and hearing by the Word of God.

Can I be sure that I have true, unfeigned faith? Yes, you can. Look at Romans 15:13. *"Now the God of hope fill you with all joy and peace in believing, that ye may abound in hope, through the power of the Holy Ghost."*

If you are fearful in any way, then you can know that you are not walking in mountain moving faith. If you are questioning what you should do in a situation, then you can know that you are not walking in the faith about which we are talking. The Word of God says that the God of hope will fill you with all joy and peace in believing.

Should I have surgery or just trust God? If you have to ask, then you are not walking in the level of faith that is needed. If there is fear, then you are not walking in the level of faith you need to move your mountain. Do **not** try to get healed on someone else's Rhema Word! Get your **own** word and let your faith arise and your enemies be scattered.

Hallelujah! Yes, God can do anything; but, we do not receive according to His ability. We receive according to our faith. True, unfeigned faith will bring joy and peace and will cause you to abound in hope. Faith, the substance of things hoped for! How will this happen? Through the power of the Holy Ghost.

Is it really that important to be **baptized** in the Holy Ghost with the evidence of speaking in tongues? Well, we are about to find out.

Chapter 7

Praying In The Spirit

Having been raised with a Full Gospel, Pentecostal background, I have never had a problem with speaking in tongues being the evidence of the baptism of the Holy Ghost. I have, however, found out through the years, that the dogma of the full gospel circles are just the rules and regulations of man. I was taught that you did not have the Spirit of God if you did not speak in tongues. That, however, is a misunderstanding of the meaning of the full counsel of God and His Word.

The Lord has said in Romans 8:9 that if we do not have the Spirit of Christ, we are not His. Well, we all know people who are born again Christians that do not speak in tongues. Therefore, there must be more to it than the obvious.

In John 6:44a it says: *"No man can come to me, except the Father which hath sent me draw him..."*

So, from this we can be assured that the

Father draws every man to Himself; then it is up to the individual to accept or reject that drawing power. If you have come to the Father, have been born again through the work of the cross through Jesus Christ, then the Spirit of Christ is in you. (Romans 8:9)

Then, what is this being endued with power from on high? *"For John truly baptized with water; but ye shall be baptized with the Holy Ghost not many days hence."* (Acts 1:5) . . .*"But ye shall receive power, after that the Holy Ghost is come upon you: and ye shall be witnesses unto me both in Jerusalem, and in all Judea, and in Samaria, and unto the uttermost part of the earth."* (Acts 1:8) . . . *"And, behold, I send the promise of my Father upon you: but tarry ye in the city of Jerusalem, until ye be endued with power from on high."* (Luke 24:49) . . . *"Even the Spirit of truth; whom the world cannot receive, because it seeth him not, neither knoweth him: but ye know him; for he dwelleth with you, and shall be in you."* (John 14:17) . . . *"Then Peter said unto them, Repent, and be baptized every one of you in the name of Jesus Christ for the remission of sins, and ye shall receive the gift of the Holy Ghost."* (Acts 2:38) He goes on to say that this promise of the Holy Ghost is to them; to their children; to their children's children; even to them that are afar off, even as many as the Lord shall call. **That's Us!**

In Acts 2:4, it says they were all filled with the Holy Ghost and began to speak in other tongues as the Spirit gave them utterance. In Acts 10, we have the story of Peter going to the house of Cornelius and the gift of the Holy Ghost was poured out on the Gentiles. How did they know this? *"For they heard them speak with tongues, and magnify God . . ."* (Acts 10:46)

I believe the Bible very plainly teaches that the gift of tongues is a manifestation of the baptism of the Holy Ghost. I also believe there are the gifts of tongues and the interpretation of those tongues that are listed with the other gifts of the Spirit. If satan can get us to believe that "tongues" is just another one of the gifts, and not everyone will speak in tongues, then he can keep you from the power of the baptism in the Holy Ghost.

Paul writes in I Corinthians 14:2 to the church in Corinth telling them, *"For he that speaketh in an unknown tongue speaketh not unto men, but unto God: for no man understandeth him; howbeit in the spirit he speaketh mysteries."* So, from this we can know that when we speak in tongues, we are

64

speaking directly to God, and no one can understand what we are saying. When satan was cast out of heaven, he lost the ability to understand the language of God. He gave up his authority to hear into God's Spirit realm with clarity and understanding. Is it any wonder that he is so vehement against God's children speaking in their heavenly language?

Paul said to the church in Corinth; I will pray with the Spirit and I will also pray with the natural understanding. We can truly have a direct line to God the Father through the Holy Spirit speaking through us. What a powerful tool against the powers of darkness!

Romans 8:26,27 gives us an awesome reason to seek after the power of speaking in tongues. *"Likewise the Spirit also helpeth our infirmities: for we know not what we should pray for as we ought: but the Spirit itself maketh intercession for us with groanings which cannot be uttered. And he that searcheth the hearts knoweth what is the mind of the Spirit, because he maketh intercession for the saints according to the will of God."* When we pray in the Spirit with groanings and utterings that cannot be understood by man (or devil), we can know that we are praying the perfect will of the Father in behalf of the need in our life. What a powerful, overcoming tool in the hands of the children of the Kingdom!

Many times I have not known the way to pray in a given situation. Especially if it concerns loved ones or our church ministry. My plan and God's plan are not always the same, as most of us have found out the hard way.

So many Christians do not know how to distinguish the difference in the voice of the Spirit; the voice of the enemy; or the voice of their own mind. Many people take just anything that flashes through their mind and call it God! Is it any wonder there is such a lack of anointing in the church of Jesus Christ today.

In his book "Praying In The Spirit," Col Stringer said something that should be used as a measuring rod for the voices we hear. He said; "There are at least three voices that can communicate with our minds, the Lord (spontaneous words that bring encouragement, edification, and correction), the devil (bringing pressure, compulsion to act, condemnation and fear), and our own thoughts (usually rational, logical, and making excuses for our shortcomings)."

The Lord tells us in I John to not believe every

spirit but to try them to see whether or not they are of God. Allowing the Holy Ghost that is in us do the talking, is a great way to know who is speaking and who is not!

Jude 20 says: *"But ye, beloved, building up yourselves on your most holy faith, praying in the Holy Ghost."* We must understand the importance of this gift from God.

1. Tongues is the key to entering the realm of the spirit.

2. Tongues is a vital key to the anointing of God being manifested in your life.

3. Tongues will affect every area of your life: Spirit, Soul, and Body. It brings edification to your spirit, truth to your mind, and life to your body.

The Lord tells us in Ephesians 3:13~16, that we are to be strengthened with might through His Spirit in our inner man. We all have pressures and trials of life that we face on a regular basis. If our inner man is not built up in the strength and power of His might, we will not be able to handle the pressure of this life. We spend time doing everything except the very thing that will bring us victory and overcoming power for life. We spend hours in the gym; hours running or doing other types of bodily exercise; all kinds of money getting the right nutrition or vitamins for our body. We will go to the beach or to the mountains to "quiet our mind" when all we really **need** to do is get our mind **renewed** in the power of the Holy Ghost!

Jesus said in John 16:13 that when He, the Spirit of truth is come, He will guide you into all truth. You mean we can know all truth! Only as we allow Him to guide us. He will not **force** us into truth. He will guide us into His truth.

Romans, the eighth chapter, gives us insight regarding the truth of walking in the Spirit. You need to read the entire chapter to get the fulness of what the Lord is trying to say. Then in Galatians 5:16 Paul writes these words of instruction, *"This I say then, Walk in the Spirit, and ye shall not fulfil the lust of the flesh."*

Can this be done? I firmly believe that only as we give the Holy Ghost preeminence in our life can this be done. Otherwise, we will continually be up and down and in and out of our spiritual experience.

In I Corinthians 14:18 Paul says: *"I thank my God, I speak with tongues more than ye all."* Remember I Corinthians 14:2 told us that he who speaks in tongues is speaking directly to God and no man can understand him; but that he is speaking **mysteries**. I believe that Paul prayed in the Holy Ghost until the **mysteries** of God became revelation in his spirit and he began to walk in a new realm of the manifestation of the glory of God.

The word "mysteries" in Greek breaks down to "that which being outside the range of unassisted natural apprehension, can be made known only by divine revelation . . . and only to those who are illuminated by His Spirit . . . its scriptural significance is truth revealed" (Vines).

Furthermore, Paul says: *"And my speech and my preaching was not with enticing words of man's wisdom, but in demonstration of the Spirit and of power: That your faith should not stand in the wisdom of men, but in the power of God. Howbeit we speak wisdom among them that are perfect: yet not the wisdom of this world, nor of the princes of this world, that come to nought: But we speak the wisdom of God in a mystery, even the hidden wisdom, which*

God ordained before the world unto our glory: which none of the princes of this world knew: for had they known it, they would not have crucified the Lord of glory." (I Cor 2:4~8) Then in verse 10 he says: *"But God hath revealed them unto us by his Spirit: for the Spirit searcheth all things, yea, the deep things of God."*

I truly believe that if we tap into the power and truths of the Holy Spirit that is available to us, there would never be a need for Spirit-filled Christians to go to the "world's" psychiatrists and psychologists. There is certainly a place for these professions; but that place is in the world, not in the church. Pastor Col Stringer said, ". . .the world is a mental hospital without walls." I am in total agreement with that statement.

Again, John 16:13 gives us an awesome promise, *"But when he, the Spirit of truth, is come, he will guide you into all truth . . ."* Please take note. He did not say He "might" do this, and He did not say that He would guide you into "part" truth! He said "when" He comes, not "if" he comes; He will "guide" not "force" you into all...all...**all** truth. I gather from this scripture, that if we connect and grasp the impact of this mighty Word of God, we can have the capabilities working within us through the power of the Holy Ghost to walk free from error. Am I preaching that we can be perfect? Not exactly. What I am preaching is that the one who is the completion of perfection desires to live and reign in our heart and spirit. If we give Him that freedom, then we can know that He has promised to lead us and guide us into all truth.

I told you previously that praying in tongues is a vital key to entering into the spirit realm. When I pray in tongues, I actually bypass my conscious mind and begin to enter into the realm of understanding the "mysteries" of God. There is a secret place we can go to and know we are in a higher place with the Lord.

Psalm 91:1 tells us, *"He that dwelleth in the secret place of the most High shall abide* (live in) *under the shadow of the Almighty."* This place is not to be kept a secret from us; it is being kept for us!

Referring again to Paul's writing to the church in Corinth, he says: *"But the natural man receiveth not the things of the Spirit of God: for they are foolishness unto him: neither can he know them, because they are spiritually discerned."* (I Cor 2:14)

The word "natural" in Greek is the word

"psuchikos" from which we get our words psychiatry and psychology. The word means "belonging to the psuche - soul, the lower part of immaterial in man, natural, physical . . . set in contrast to pneumatikos, or spiritual" (Vines).

Therefore, this scripture is telling us that the "natural" man is operating out of his head or worldly wisdom and cannot know the things of the Spirit. If we speak of spirits to a worldly person, he will think we are referring to spirits such as Jack Daniels or Jim Beam.

I cannot pass up this opportunity to relate a story that happened to us on a trip one time. This truth of knowing about spirits can work in the other way as well. We were returning home from a ministry trip on which our daughter, Ginger, and our two grandchildren, Tiffany and Wesley, were able to be with us. Now, you need to understand, Ginger was raised in a Christian home and, by the grace of God, was never in the world. We went into a restaurant for breakfast on our way home. Our waiter seemed to be a little out of sorts, from the taking of our order, to the bringing of our food. I had asked for some bread, which he had neglected to get for me. He apologized and went to get it. Upon his return, he had two slices of bread just lying on the tray he was carrying. He proceeded to pick it up with his bare hands and hand it to me. I was taken back to say the least. He really seemed to be pre-occupied as I made the statement that it was a good thing that I asked the Lord to bless our food. He proceeded to apologize again and said he had a rough night sitting up with his friend, Jim Beam. As he left the table, I was grumbling about the poor service when Ginger spoke up and said; "We really have to feel sorry for the poor guy. After all, he sat up all night with his sick friend." Well, needless to say, Bob, Mikki, and I almost fell off our chairs laughing at her naivete. She did not know that Jim Beam was an alcoholic drink. Our two grandchildren were totally in the dark as well as to our reason for hysterical laughter. I guess there is a good side to not recognizing the spirits!

We can have that inner voice, that "unction from the Holy One to know all things," concerning the things of the Spirit. But if we are not filled with the Spirit, we can be led astray. That tells me that if we are filled with the Spirit, we can trust Him to lead us and guide us into **all truth**.

Again, tongues is a vital key to the anointing of

God being manifested in our life. It will affect every area of your life if we will just give Him free reign to do so.

If Paul, who was the greatest apostle that ever lived and one who God entrusted with the greatest portion of the New Testament recording of the Word of God, needed to say; "I thank my God that I pray in tongues more than any of you," then it must certainly be of utmost importance for us to consider it to be a vital need in our spiritual walk with the Lord. I know from personal experience that when I found myself at a loss for words as to how to pray, and I allowed the Holy Spirit to speak through me; the answers came. Praise His Holy Name!!!

The Spirit of God is resident within us and we must learn to trust in that voice and become sensitive to His leading us into all truth.

I Corinthians 14:4 says: *"He who speaks in tongues edifies himself."* The word "edify" means to charge up, like you would charge up a run down battery. It also means a powerful surge of vitality. Many times I have been exhausted physically, mentally, and emotionally. I entered into that secret place with the Lord and began to pray in the Spirit and came out of that place with the Holy Ghost of

God, refreshed and revitalized in His power and might. Praying in tongues **works** . . . Let it!!

Can I explain it? No! Can I with my natural mind understand it? No! Can I tell you exactly how it works? No! But, neither can I tell you how electricity works; yet, I still turn on my light switch to dispel the darkness. I cannot begin to understand the computer, but I still use it. I cannot for the life of me understand how a brown cow can eat green grass and give us white milk, but I continue to enjoy what I do not understand.

Are you getting the message? Do not try so hard to understand the things of the Spirit with the natural mind. It just will not work! Just receive it by faith and enjoy the fruit of His promises.

It has been said by the world and the "religious" community that tongues is an escape from reality. Well, I guess in a way, they are right. It is called "walking in the spirit and not fulfilling the lusts of the flesh."

We are not "earthly beings having a temporary spiritual experience." We are "spiritual beings having a temporary earthly experience!" I am in this world, but not **of** this world. Hallelujah! Ephesians 5:17~20 gives us words of instructions by which to live. *"Wherefore be ye not unwise, but understanding what the will of the Lord is. And be not drunk with wine, wherein is excess; but be filled with the Spirit; Speaking to yourselves in psalms and hymns and spiritual songs, singing and making melody in your heart to the Lord; Giving thanks always for all things unto God and the Father in the name of our Lord Jesus Christ."*

Speaking to yourself with psalms and hymns and spiritual songs; singing and making melody in your heart to the Lord . . .Talk to ourself! Wouldn't the "world's system" have a time with that? We can do something on purpose that will bring us into a new place with the Lord and cause us to be an overcomer and victorious in every area of our life.

It is known as "praying in the spirit." There is another way that I have learned through years of experience that will bring results through prayer. It is what I call "breakthrough prayers."

Chapter 8

Breakthrough Prayers

What exactly do we mean by "breakthrough prayers?" I found this to be an interesting insight. The word, breakthrough, in Webster's New World Dictionary says this:

1. the act, result, or place of breaking through against resistance, as in warfare.
2. a strikingly important advance or discovery.

Now do you get the understanding of what I mean when I say "breakthrough prayers"? We must get power through the Word of God to advance the Kingdom of God through our receiving a revelation of praying not just words, but **the** Word. The Word of God, the written logos Word of God, will bring with it a "strikingly important discovery" of the ability we are given to break through the lines of the enemy by praying the Word of God. I am going to give you some personal examples of the power in praying the

Word of God. James 5:16 tells us that "the effectual, fervent prayer of a righteous man avails much." In plain English, we have to be really serious about what we are praying. The effectual, fervent prayer! We also have to be living a righteous life in Christ. That simply means we are in right standing with Him.

You cannot expect the Lord to answer the prayers of one who is doing his own thing, living a life of sin and corruption with the world. Then, when something happens that he is not able to fix, he runs to God for help. That is **not** the way it works.

I minister in prisons quite often, and we see what is called "jail-house conversions." As long as they are behind bars, God is their lifeline. But, as soon as they are out, they go right back to doing their own thing. That is **not** true conversion! That is a spiritual "quick fix," and it will not last if there has not been a true heart change.

John 9:31 says: *"Now we know that God heareth not sinners: but if any man be a worshipper of God, and doeth his will, him he heareth."* The prayers of a sinner that the Lord hears are prayers of repentance; then comes the obedience aspect of doing His will. So, having said that, what are some of those "word" prayers that work?

One that I truly believe is a most powerful prayer for those who have loved ones that are lost, is found in II Corinthians 4:3,4. *"But if our gospel be hid, it is hid to them that are lost: In whom the god of this world hath blinded the minds of them which believe not, lest the light of the glorious gospel of Christ, who is the image of God, should shine unto them."* If our loved one cannot hear the gospel of Jesus Christ, then it is because their minds have been blinded by the god of this world. That is what the Word says!

Begin to pray this scripture over them. I have seen this work time and time again as I shared this truth with those that have sons and daughters or a spouse that is not open to hear the Word of the Lord. I tell them: "stop talking to **them** about the Lord, and start talking to the **Lord** about them." Pray the Word of God over them.

For example: "Lord, my son,_____, just has no heart to hear or receive your plan of salvation. Lord, I know your Word says if the Gospel is hid, it is hidden to them that are lost because the god of this world has blinded their minds so they cannot see what you have for them. So, Lord, I ask you now to unblind their mind that the god of this world has blinded, and set them free in their own will to be open to hear and receive your Word into their life. According to II Corinthians 4:3~4, I ask for your light of this glorious Gospel to shine unto them that they might be saved. I believe that I have a promise of household salvation given unto me through your Word. Lord, the apostle Paul told the jailor that he and his family would be saved if he would believe upon the Lord Jesus Christ. What was good for the jailor in Acts 16:31, is good for me and my house." Hallelujah!

When our son, John, was just out of high school and starting out on his own, he started dating a young woman that I strongly felt in my spirit was not the right one for him. She was a beautiful Christian girl, but I had this "mom" thing happening, so I went to the Lord on his behalf. John was going through that "I'm an adult" thing, and Mom's input into his social life was not high on his agenda.

He had gone out with this young woman several times and things seemed to be looking a little too serious from my standpoint. So I got into the Word for some instructions. In Proverbs 3:3, I found the following: *"Let not mercy and truth forsake thee:*

bind them about thy neck; write them upon the table of thine heart." I began to pray that the Lord would do just that; send His mercy and truth to my son John and bind them around his neck so that he would not be able to get away from the truths and instructions of the Word of God.

I saw in Psalm 37:23 that, *"The steps of a good man are ordered by the Lord: and he delighteth in his way."* I knew that my son was a "good" man and that the Lord had His hand upon him and desired to order his steps. I also believed that John did delight in the ways of the Lord, even though (at this time in his life) that fact seemed to be a little distant. I continued to pray the Word of God over his life and waited for the Lord to give me further instructions. I never once told John to **not** date that girl anymore. Still, a funny thing happened one night. I was in prayer about this situation when John came in very early from his date. He stuck his head in the door and said, "Mom, will you stop praying for me!"

I never did find out what happened on that date, but I do know it was the **last** date that John had with that girl. He went on to marry the one the Lord had planned from the foundation of the world, and DeAnna Lynn Elliott became our daughter. They now pastor "The Father's House." You see, their steps are ordered by God!

Praying the Word works! Breakthrough prayers will not only change your life, but the lives of your loved ones as well. One of the current prayers that is changing lives is known as the "Prayer of Jabez." Dr. Bruce Wilkinson, founder and president of "Walk Through The Bible" ministries, wrote a book entitled, "The Prayer of Jabez," and it has been used by God to change literally thousands of lives throughout the world. I know it changed mine. It is based upon the scripture found in I Chronicles 4:10. *"And Jabez called on the God of Israel, saying, Oh that thou wouldest bless me indeed, and enlarge my coast, and that thine hand might be with me, and that thou wouldest keep me from evil, that it may not grieve me! And God granted him that which he requested."* The Holy Bible, New King James Version (NKJV),(c) 1984 by Thomas Nelson Publishing, says it this way; *"And Jabez called on the God of Israel saying, 'Oh, that You would bless me indeed, and enlarge my territory, that Your hand would be with me, and that You would keep me from evil, that I may not cause pain!' So God granted him his request."* I read this little book and began to pray that little prayer; I want to tell you it has changed my life! I am experiencing the blessings of God in a new way. I am walking in a new realm of revelation of the power of the Word of God and the authority it has on this earth as it is prayed or spoken with faith. I have seen, first hand, it change the lives of those around me that began to walk in the promises of God and pray **the** Word, not just pray words.

What is the key to praying the Word instead of just praying words? Get in the Bible and find the scripture that relates to your situation or problem, such as household salvation or health. Then begin to pray that Word of God until it goes from just being logos (written word) to Rhema (living word) in your spirit. There is a promise to stand on in every book of the Bible. You can start at Genesis and end at the book of Revelation and find a promise of God that will be a right now applicable Word for your life!

One of my very favorites in the Old Testament is Joshua 1:8~9. *"This book of the law shall not depart out of thy mouth; but thou shalt meditate therein day and night, that thou mayest observe to do according to all that is written therein: for then thou shalt make thy way prosperous, and then thou shalt have good success. Have not I commanded thee? Be strong and of a good courage; be not afraid, neither be thou dismayed: for the Lord thy God is with thee whithersoever thou goest."* What an awesome promise from the creator of the universe!

We have all heard of the thirty, sixty, and one hundred-fold blessing. But my prayer for God's blessing on my life is Deuteronomy 1:11. *"The Lord God of your fathers make you a thousand times so many more as ye are, and bless you, as he hath promised you!"*

One of my New Testament favorites is I John 5:13~15. This is a powerful declaration of what is rightfully ours as a child of God. *"These things have I written unto you that believe on the name of the Son of God; that ye may know that ye have eternal life, and that ye may believe on the name of the Son of God. And this is the confidence that we have in him, that, if we ask anything according to his will, he heareth us: And if we know that he hear us, whatsoever we ask, we know that we have the petitions that we desired of him."* Are we getting this? Do we really understand the power that we are talking about here? Can we possibly comprehend that the Ancient of Days, the one that spoke the worlds into being, has given unto us these promises. Isaiah 55:11 says: *"So shall my word be that goeth forth out of my mouth: it shall not return unto me void, but it shall accomplish that which I please, and it shall prosper in the thing whereto I sent it."*

We **really** need to get a grip here! God **cannot** lie and His Word will do what He said it will do!!! It's time to start praying the Word and see it do what the Lord said it would do!

It's Time! It's Time! **It's Time!**

Do you really mean business with God? Do you really want to see His hand move in your life like I am talking about? Do you really want to experience the presence of God in your life like you have never before experienced? Then I have a suggestion for you. . . Get in the Word of God, go through it chapter by chapter, book by book and find the promises to pray that He has for you.

If that seems too overwhelming, then go to the Christian Bookstore and get a book of the promises of God. Begin to pray the Word instead of **just** praying words. I can guarantee it will change your life! The Lord wants us, as His children, to realize that He is calling us to a higher place in Him. In order to get there, we **must** be willing to go beyond where we are now, to where we have never been. He wants to truly "open the windows of heaven" and pour out a blessing that we will not be able to contain.

I do not know about you, but I, for one, am saying to the Lord, "show me your ways, Lord. I want to see your face. Take me up higher in You, Lord." What is the key to going up yet another step in Him?

Several years ago, I did a conference on "Praise and Worship" The Key That Unlocks The Door. I believe this to be even more true today than it was then. We cannot get into His realm without learning about praise and worship.

Chapter 9

Opening The Windows Of Heaven

The Lord spoke to us in Acts 15:16 with the following words, *"After this I will return, and will build again the tabernacle of David, which is fallen down; and I will build again the ruins thereof, and I will set it up."* In Amos 9:11~13, He says this, *"In that day will I raise up the tabernacle of David that is fallen, and close up the breaches thereof; and I will raise up his ruins, and I will build it as in the days of old: That they may possess the remnant of Edom, and of all the heathen, which are called by my name, saith the Lord that doeth this. Behold, the days come, saith the Lord, that the plowman shall overtake the reaper, and the treader of grapes him that soweth seed; and the mountains shall drop sweet wine, and all the hills shall melt."*

We all know that the Tabernacle of David was a house of worship. We also know that music played an important part in David's life. We can read in

I Samuel 16 how God used David's playing his harp to drive away the evil spirits from King Saul. Worship has power.

For so long the Lord has desired to raise up the Tabernacle of David, or restore to His church the power of worship. This is His plan for **this** generation; to have the Tabernacle of David restored; to have the power of praise and true worship come up before His "throne of grace" and return to the earth as His hand upon the church of the living God. For so long the world has looked upon the modern day church in mockery. For so many years, the power has been so insignificant, that it made very little lasting impact upon a world of sin and sickness. **But that is about to change!** The power of the resurrection is about to be seen upon this earth. The power of the Word of God is about to be unleashed in the church of the living God; the power of **worship** is about to change our world.

This will happen whether we are a part of it or not; this will happen! The Lord wants us to begin to realize the power He has given us through praise and worship. He is calling His intercessors to become true worshippers.

Jesus said to the woman at the well; you do

not know what you worship (paraphrase, John 4:22). But, the hour is coming, and now is when the **true** worshipper shall worship the Father in spirit and in truth: for the Father seeketh such to worship Him. This is the Tabernacle of David being restored. True worship must become a reality before the plowman can begin to overtake the reaper; and the harvest become more than we can comprehend.

II Chronicles 5:13~14 says: *"It came even to pass, as the trumpeters and singers were as one, to make one sound to be heard in praising and thanking the Lord; and when they lifted up their voice with the trumpets and cymbals and instruments of music, and praised the Lord, saying, For He is good; for His mercy endureth forever: that then the house was filled with a cloud, even the house of the Lord; So that the priests could not stand to minister by reason of the cloud: for the Glory of the Lord had filled the house of God."* We must realize that when this happens, the **miracles** will be there, the **deliverances** will be there, the **healings** will be there. When Jesus shows up in this kind of manifested power, **something** is going to happen! It will not be man; it will not be woman; it will not even be the music . . . it will be the result of true worship and the welcoming presence of the Holy

Spirit. **It's Time!** Habakkuk 2:1~3 says: *"I will stand upon my watch, and set me upon the tower, and will watch to see what he will say unto me, and what I shall answer when I am reproved. And the Lord answered me, and said, Write the vision, and make it plain upon tables, that he may run that readeth it. For the vision is yet for an appointed time, but at the end it shall speak, and not lie: though it tarry, wait for it; because it will surely come, it will not tarry."*

It's Time. It's time to run with the truth of the Word of God; it's time to run with the power of His presence of the glory of the Lord to be in our midst. It's time for the plowman to overtake the reaper and the treader of grapes him that soweth the seed! My heart yearns for those that I minister to; for them to become enriched and fired up with the presence of the Lord in their lives, that they pass me by with the anointing of God being manifested in and through them. As I look at the lives I minister to on a regular basis, I can see the various stages of growth and spiritual advancement. How can that be discerned? Through the degree of hunger for worship and by the fruit that is being manifested in their lives. The Lord so wants to **open the windows of heaven**, and pour out His blessings upon His children. But, how do we open the windows of heaven? Psalm 100:4 gives us a little insight into entering the presence of the Lord. *"Enter into his gates with thanksgiving, and into his courts with praise: be thankful unto him, and bless his name."* From this scripture we can surmise that thanksgiving will get the gates open; praise will move us into His courts; but **worship** will get us His undivided attention. From the very beginning, all He ever wanted was a people who would love and worship Him just for who He is.

In his book "God's Favorite House, Tommy Tenney said this:

The Word of God tells us that there are five distinct and definite things that open the windows of heaven. This isn't a formula; it is a lifestyle of worship and dedication to God first in all things. All of the following are various elements of worship.

1. *Tithing* is an ancient key to the heavenlies that even predates the giving of the law to Abraham. The principle of giving God the "firstfruits" of our income or increase is clearly described in the book of Malachi: *"Bring all the tithes into the storehouse, that there may be*

food in My house, and try Me now is this," says the Lord of hosts, "If I will not open for you the windows of heaven and pour out for you such blessing that there will not be room enough to receive it." (Malachi 3:10 NKJV)

The Lord tells us in Proverbs 3:9, *"Honour the Lord with thy substance, and with the firstfruits of all thine increase."* Pastor Tenney went on to say:

2. *Persecution* also opens the heavens as demonstrated in the book of Acts when Stephen was martyred: *"But he, being full of the Holy Spirit, gazed into heaven and saw the glory of God, and Jesus standing at the right hand of God, and said, 'Look! I see the heavens opened and the Son of Man standing at the right hand of God!' Then they cried out with a loud voice . . . and they cast him out of the city and stoned him."* (Acts 7:55~58a NKJV)

We can be assured, if we see Jesus standing up in our behalf, something is about to happen! Continuing with Pastor Tenney's book:

3. Persistence is an effective tool for "prying open" the gates of Heaven. Elijah prayed seven times and kept sending his servant back to search the skies until, on the seventh time, the

servant saw a cloud the size of a man's hand rise from the sea. That tiny cloud from God grew into such a powerful storm that the skies were turned black with rain and wind. (I Kings 18:42~45) Jesus told His disciples that the "door" would be opened to those who persistently ask, seek, and knock on God's door. (Matthew 7:7~8)

4. *Unity* will open the windows of heaven; it invites God's presence wherever two or three *agree* "concerning anything they ask." Jesus literally said, "For where two or three are gathered together in My name, I am there in the midst of them." (Matthew 18:19~20) The opposite side of this principle is illustrated in Peter's warning to husbands and wives to remain united so their "prayers may not be hindered." (I Peter 3:7)

5. *Worship* is the fifth key to the third heaven. David the psalmist prophesied, "Lift up your heads, O ye gates; and be ye lift up, ye everlasting doors; and the King of Glory shall come in." (Psalm 24:7) Have you ever seen a head on a gate? It is obvious that David was referring to people as "gates" and "everlasting

doors" through which the King of Glory can come to the earth. This is a call to worship."

I have just quoted Pastor Tommy Tenney from his book, "God's Favorite House" pages 42 and 43. I truly believe that God is speaking to His children around the world to come into that place of intimacy with Him that will take us into the Holy of Holies. When this happens in the church, the Tabernacle of David will be restored.

In Revelation 8:1~5 we see something happening in the Heavens that is a direct result of something that first happened on earth: *"And when he had opened the seventh seal, there was a silence in heaven about the space of half an hour. And I saw the seven angels which stood before God; and to them were given seven trumpets. And another angel came and stood at the altar, having a golden censor; and there was given unto him much incense, that he should offer it with the prayers of all saints upon the golden altar which was before the throne. And the smoke of the incense, which came with the prayers of the saints, ascended up before God out of the angel's hand. And the angel took the censor, and filled it with fire of the altar, and cast it into the earth: and there were voices, and thunderings, and lightnings, and an earthquake."* That word "prayers" in verse three, is the same as the word "worship." Psalm 141:2 says: *"Let my prayer be set forth before thee as incense; and the lifting up of my hands as the evening sacrifice."* Do you want to open the windows of heaven? Then rebuild the Tabernacle of David with your worship.

It's Time! It's Time! It's Time!

Remember what the Lord told us in Amos 9:11a: *"In that day will I raise up the tabernacle of David that is fallen. . ."* For the windows of Heaven to be opened; for the Body of Christ to begin to walk in what I am talking about; for the Glory of God to be seen on this earth, it will have to be:

The House That God Built!

Chapter 10

The House That God Built

From the time I was young, I knew God had a plan for my life. I started teaching the little kids in Sunday School when I was 12 years old. I was already teaching kids older than myself, when my Grandpa Green needed a teacher for the young adults. He simply said, "you can do it." I received prophecy after prophecy telling me what great and mighty things the Lord had in store for me. By the time our family started the Soul Seekers Gospel Group in 1974, I **knew** God had great things planned for my future.

For several years, we traveled and ministered on the weekends; came home early on Monday morning and went to our respective jobs. We won singing contests, did recording projects, appeared on radio and television programs, and had fun just spreading the Gospel and traveling all over the country. The group first consisted of my two sisters, my brother, my mother, Bob and myself. Then, later, our daughter, Ginger; our son, John, and his wife, DeAnna; my sister, Judy; Bob and me. During this time, there were others that came and went in the group. The Lord then called various members of the group out into other works, and by 1989, I knew the Lord was leading in another direction. By now, I had been preaching the Word and doing seminars and conferences for a few years. Bob and I both worked at the local Christian television station, and life was wonderful. The Lord then spoke to me a prophetic word that I **knew** would forever change my life. He told me that there would be three major changes:

1. In our church family
2. In our ministry
3. In my job

I did not want **any** of these things to change, but I knew I was hearing God speak. Within a matter of weeks, all three of these changes had taken place. I found myself at home, talking to the Lord, and making **my** plans. I had left my job at the television station and was seeking God for the next step. All of this had taken place so quickly, I just knew any day I would receive that phone call or that letter of invitation to do the "really big thing" that would catapult me into the arena of having a worldwide ministry. Days went by; then weeks; then months; and **finally**, in my state of anger, disappointment, resentment, feelings of total abandonment, and financial distress, I decided to take matters into my own hands. I could make things happen.

After all, I knew more preachers than most people ever hear of and they would be more than happy to book us for a revival or gospel sing. I picked up the phone to start making contacts, when it was as though a bolt of lightning knocked the phone out of my hand and left me shaking from head to toe. The Lord spoke to my heart that day and let me know that I had been in control long enough. Through the years, I had made the plans, booked the events, planned the trips, and prepared the messages. He had honored that time in my life, but **now**, He was about to make the changes that were necessary to get me where I needed to be in Him.

I had truly enjoyed my life (for the most part) up to this point in time; yet, there was always that little thing prodding my spirit that there must surely be more than what I had. The time had come in my life that I had to be totally honest with me, myself, and I; and then the Lord could do something in and through me. The Lord spoke to me that day as I lay on my face in my living room; I had done it long enough. It was time for me to let go and let God do it. He spoke to my heart and told me I had to be willing to "lay down" everything!

I had to be willing to "lay down" my ministry! I had to be willing to "lay down" my music! I had to be willing to "lay down" my song writing! My family! My finances! My teaching! **My Everything!!**

I was, as far as ministering was concerned, spiritually locked in my house for a year with no open doors; no new songs; no inspiration; and no invitations to go anywhere. This was so foreign to all we had known for over 15 years, and I was emotionally devastated. Still, I knew it was the hand of the Lord working in my life. My strength came from my close intercessors that came almost daily to meet with me and the Lord. Mikki Holdeman had started playing the keyboard for us after my sister, Judy, left the group. She came almost every day to learn our songs and hear the plans of the Lord being manifested to us. My close friend, Dana Meger, was also a part of that intense training in hearing and discerning the voice of the Lord. We heard the Lord speak during this time in so many ways, with so much power, that all of our lives were forever changed by the end of the year. He gave us prophetic words of encouragement, exhortation, and promise for things to come. But through all of this experience, the number one thing that I kept getting in my spirit was that the Lord had to build the house, or it would not stand. Psalm 127:1 says: *"Except the Lord build the house, they labour in vain that built it: except the Lord keep the city, the watchman waketh but in vain."* I really like the way the Message Bible says it: *"If God doesn't build the house, the builders only build shacks. If God doesn't guard the city, the night watchman might as well nap."*

For too long, the body of Christ has just been building shacks. Here today and gone tomorrow! Isaiah 43:18~19 says this: *"Remember ye not the former things, neither consider the things of old. Behold, I will do a new thing; now it shall spring forth; shall ye not know it? I will even make a way in the wilderness, and rivers in the desert."* Haggai 2:9 says: *"The glory of this latter house shall be greater than of the former, saith the Lord of hosts: and in this place will I give peace, saith the Lord of hosts."*

What place is the Lord talking about? In the latter house. He **is** doing a "new" thing, and His question is still the same! Will you know when it happens? Will you recognize My hand moving in your midst, or will you still be so locked into the "old" way that the "new" way will be missed? The glory of God's house will be greater in this last day move than in all the other moves of God put together. What an awesome thought!

I have seen the hand of God do some great and mighty things, but I know the best is yet to come. In John 1:14 the Lord says this: *"And the Word was made flesh, and dwelt among us, and we beheld his glory, the glory as of the only begotten of the Father, full of grace and truth."* Then in Ephesians 2:19~22: *"Now therefore ye are no more strangers and foreigners, but fellow citizens with the saints, and of the household of God; And are built upon the foundation of the apostles and prophets, Jesus Christ himself being the chief corner stone; In whom all the building fitly framed together groweth unto an holy temple in the Lord: In whom ye also are builded together for an habitation of God through the Spirit."*

The Lord is building His house! He is coming back for a place that is more glorious and powerful than the thing He left behind. His temple will be raised up incorruptible and holy and righteous in Him. *"What? know ye not that your body is the temple of the Holy Ghost which is in you, which ye have of God, and ye are not your own? For ye are bought with a price: therefore glorify God in your body, and in your spirit, which are God's."* (I Corinthians 6:19~20)

We have tried for so long to get everything just right so God can use us in a mighty way. Now, do not get me wrong, we need to do our very best for the glory of God, and we need to have our attitudes and morals and ethics be pleasing to the Lord; but, the Lord also wants us to realize that it is **He** who builds the house. He has already paid for the temple materials through His work on the cross. He has already laid the foundation for this Holy Temple to be built on. All we have to do is allow that Tabernacle of David, through our pure heart and clean hands, to be established in us, and He **will** use us for the glory of His Kingdom.

Once I realized that the Lord had His hand on my life from the foundation of the world and that His plan would unfold and be revealed, I was relieved of all pressure to "measure up;" to perform; to be good enough to "draw" the crowd. I know the Lord is using me, whether it's to three people or to 3,000 people. All I have to do is put into my spirit the Word of God; worship Him in spirit and in truth; obey what I know to do; then allow the Holy Ghost to take over and do what He wants to do. If I put it in, He will bring it out! Once the revelation hit me that I couldn't make it happen, I began to walk in the freedom of seeking His face. I cannot get anyone healed; but, I know the man that can. I cannot get anyone delivered from drugs or sexual sins or destructive lifestyles; but, I know the man that can. I am **not** Holy Ghost, Jr.! **What freedom!**

Joshua said, in plain english, "you can do whatever you want to do, but as for me and my house, we will serve the Lord." (Joshua 24:15)

We can relate that to his literal family, but remember, the Lord told us that our body is the temple of the Holy Ghost. We are the house of the Lord. I am determined that as for **my house**, I will serve the Lord. I will allow the Lord to build the house; and I will see His glory manifested in my life. We use to sing an old gospel song that said, "It's not my brother, not my sister, but me Oh Lord, standing in the need of prayer." Once we realize that truth, then the Lord has some building material to work with, Hallelujah!!

Through the years, I have seen ministries come and go. I have seen what seemed to be nothing more than flesh draw huge crowds, collect massive offerings, and live a life of immorality and sin outside the walls of ministry. But the Lord says, "fret not, My Word is true. If I did not build the house, it will fall. It will crumble and the noise of it's fall will be great." But there is a people who are being raised up in incorruption and God's love, that will change the world in which we live. It's Time!!

I, like Joshua, by the grace of God, intend to be one of them. What will it take to be a part of this group of people? What is the price for the anointing of God that we are talking about? Are we willing to pay the price?

This is a costly anointing!

Chapter 11

What Is The Cost?

Through the years, I have met so many people that wanted to do a work for the Lord; to be in an "up front" position. Yet, they are not willing to spend the time necessary in the Word of God, or in the presence of the Lord, to get what they need to be equipped to minister to the needs of others. They view the life of ministry as one of glamour and excitement. It can be that, at times, but the truth of the matter is if you do not know how to cast all your cares upon Him, it can be a life of disillusionment with people; with the "system" of church doctrine; and one of discouragement real quick.

Most of these people that I am talking about have the wrong motivation and wrong attitude. If they do get in a place or position of leadership, it is usually through a spirit of manipulation. They live out their ministry filled with insecurity, which opens them up to fear. These spirits working through them will in turn give birth to a spirit of intimidation and control. I talked in the last chapter about God building the house, and about how if He does not build it, then the labor is in vain. Let's look now, at the price of this Holy Temple of God.

Several years ago, when I was working at the Christian television station, one of my jobs was to schedule guests for a live program they called the 12:20 Club. This was built around the scripture in I Corinthians 12:20, that says we are many members, yet one body. The host of the program was Pastor Joe Brainard from a Baptist church. He loved the body of Christ and was so excited about this pilot ship program that the Lord was raising up. He had a vision from God to see the body of Christ brought together and the walls of tradition and religion brought down by the power of Christ.

I had scheduled a local pastor to be his guest on the program this one particular day. He was a little late arriving at the studio, so they did not have the opportunity to talk before going on the air "live." As Pastor Joe started out this interview, he asked the guest pastor what seemed to be a very simple and basic question. "What is the Lord doing in your church?" The pastor looked at him and, on live television replied, "Oh, not much." Needless to say, Pastor Joe was stunned at the reply and, being new to live television, suffered a slight lull in the opening conversation and resorted to music to fill the gap. After the program was over, they had a private conversation and Pastor Joe asked him when he felt the call of God on his life to be a pastor. This man then said, "Oh, I don't really know that I was ever, what you would say, "called" to do what I am doing. I was simply too weak physically to do manual labor, and wasn't smart enough to be a doctor or lawyer, so I decided to go to Bible School. It seemed to be the easiest profession for me to get into." I could not comprehend this entire conversation, and I am sure Pastor Joe, being the good Baptist that he was, could not either.

I have no way of knowing, but I can almost guarantee that this man is no longer pastoring a church, or if he is, he is one miserable man unless the Lord has done a mighty work in his life.

What is it going to cost us to be a temple of ministry that God builds?

Called!

The number one thing to this kind of life, whether you are a minister or just a child of God that wants to be all He has called you to be, is to **know** He has called you! Exactly what does it mean to be called? We know in the parable of the marriage feast Jesus said, *"Many are called, but few are chosen."* (Matthew 22:14)

In the natural, we can look at being called as: a ministry; a vocation; our walk in life; or many other things. But for the purpose of this message, and the point I want to make, let's look to the Word. I Peter 1:15 lets us know **who** has called us! *"But as he which hath called you is holy, so be ye holy in all manner of conversation."* The Most Holy One has called us . . . and because of that we are to be holy (righteous, upright, pure, blameless), in everything we do.

What has He called us to or from, as the case may be? *"But ye are a chosen generation, a royal priesthood, an holy nation, a peculiar people; that ye should show forth the praises of Him who hath called you out of darkness into His marvelous light."* (I Peter 2:9)

What are the results of this calling? *"Behold, what manner of love the Father hath bestowed upon us, that we should be called the sons of God: therefore the world knoweth us not, because it knew him not."* (I John 3:1) Because we have been called out of darkness, we are now called, His sons . . . answering that call, is what will make you a "chosen one" that Jesus talked about in Matthew. So, you feel like you have answered that call, and want to become all that the Lord has said you can be. What is next?

Consecrated!

This is mostly Old Testament terminology. Aaron and his sons were "consecrated" unto the Lord (Exodus 29:29). This term usually meant to be set apart, or wholly given unto something. Only that which was purified and consecrated could be offered to the Lord. Under the new covenant a better way was provided. In the book of Hebrews, chapter ten, you can read where Jesus broke through the veil that separated man from God and gave His flesh so you and I can be fully consecrated to Him (I encourage you to read that entire passage to get a fuller understanding of what we have in Christ).

"I beseech you therefore, brethren, by the mercies of God, that ye present your bodies a living

sacrifice, holy, acceptable unto God, which is your reasonable service. And be not conformed to this world: but be ye transformed by the renewing of your mind, that you may prove what is that good, and acceptable, and perfect will of God." (Romans 12:1~2)

Please take notice that the Lord calls this our "reasonable" service. If we are consecrated wholly unto Him, we will be able to prove what is His will for our life. So far we have received and responded to the call of God; we have made a decision to consecrate ourselves unto Him. Now what?

Committed!

Committed means "dedicated to." With true commitment comes responsibility. When you get married, you take vows before God and man to "commit" your heart and soul to the one you love. You become "dedicated" to the task of pleasing your spouse. With that commitment, comes the responsibility of fulfillment. Husbands are expected to take care of their families need; food, clothing, etc. A woman is expected to be a wife and mother to her home and children. Now don't get me wrong; a woman or a man for that matter, can take on any of the responsibilities of the home or the work force, if they are in harmony and agreement with one another. In the realm of the spirit, we accept Jesus; become His bride; then He directs us to our spiritual home (or place of gathering) to worship Him. As we grow in our relationship with the Lord, we then desire to do more to please Him. We may take on the job of cleaning the church, leading the worship, or being an usher or greeter at the door. "Oh well, it's just standing at the door, or passing the offering plate!" No! It is called commitment!

In Matthew 25:14~30, we have the story of the talents. We all know this story, but I just want to point out one thing in particular to you. The one who was given the last talent, hid it in the earth and reaped absolutely nothing for the Lord, was **not** in right relationship! There was no commitment! *"Then he which had received the one talent came and said, Lord, I knew thee that thou art an hard man, reaping where thou hast not sown, and gathering where thou hast not strewed: And I was afraid, and went and hid thy talent in the earth: lo, there thou hast that is thine."* (Matthew 25:24~25)

He said he knew the Lord was a hard man and he feared not measuring up! He hid the talent in the earth; "the flesh." But, what was the response of the master? In verse 26, he tells him that he is "wicked and lazy. If you had been 'truly committed' to pleasing me, you have at least have put forth some effort to bless me." What then is the final outcome of being Called, Consecrated, and Committed?

We have already looked at John 3:1, but let's go on and see what the Lord has to say in the next verses: *"Beloved, now are we the sons of God, and it doth not yet appear what we shall be: but we know that, when he shall appear, we shall be like him; for we shall see him as he is. And every man that hath this hope in him purifieth himself, even as he is pure."* (I John 3:2~3)

This scripture just said that all of us who have this hope in us, will purify ourselves, so we can in turn, be pure like the Lord is pure. The bottom line is, if you desire to have this scripture fulfilled in you, and to see Him as He is, then you will become:

Called, Consecrated, and Committed!!

Does this have the ring of "righteousness" to it? As my grandchildren say; "It's like . . ." righteousness. How do we get there? Next chapter!

Chapter 12

Established In Righteousness

Isaiah 54:14 says this: *"In righteousness shalt thou be established: thou shalt be far from oppression; for thou shalt not fear: and from terror; for it shall not come near thee."*

We are to be established in righteousness. How can we possibly do this? How can we ever hope to attain what this Word is speaking to us? The bottom line is; We Can't! Within our own strengths and abilities we cannot; but, Jesus made a way. I am going to give you a lot of scripture in this chapter and I encourage you to **not** skip over it thinking you already "know" this part. It is only through the Word of God that we can ever hope to attain this righteousness. Keep in mind, we are being told to get established in righteousness. II Corinthians 5:21 tells us how this is done: *"For he hath made him to be sin for us, who knew no sin; that we might be made the righteousness of God in him."* Just think about what this scripture has said! Jesus took our sin, and gave us His righteousness. Does that boggle your mind, or what? That tells us **what** happened. Now look at Romans 3:21~22. This tells us **when** and **who**: *"But now the righteousness of God without the law is manifested, being witnessed by the law and the prophets; Even the righteousness of God which is by faith of Jesus Christ unto all and upon all them that believe: for there is no difference."*

When does this take place? When we, by faith, believe upon the Lord Jesus Christ. And who is this for? All them that believe, for there is no difference. No difference in what? No difference between the Jew and the Gentile. If we are in Christ, then we are Abraham's seed and heirs according to the promise of God! (Galatians 3:29) Our next question is **how**? *"And if Christ be in you, the body is dead because of sin; but the Spirit is life because of righteousness."* (Romans 8:10)

Paul is speaking to the church in Galatia and gives them these words of instruction: *"O foolish Galatians, who hath bewitched you, that ye should not obey the truth, before whose eyes Jesus Christ hath been evidently set forth, crucified among you? This only would I learn of you, Received ye the Spirit*

114

by the works of the law, or by the hearing of faith?
Are ye so foolish? having begun in the Spirit, are ye
now made perfect by the flesh?" (Galatians 3:1~3)
Paul is, in essence, saying to them; do you think you
can do something greater and accomplish more
through the works of your flesh than what you have
freely received by faith through the work that Jesus
Christ has done for you? He goes even further with
his instruction in chapter five, verse one, saying this:
"Stand fast therefore in the liberty wherewith Christ
hath made us free, and be not entangled again with
the yoke of bondage."

The Lord has given me a great revelation! If we
are going to be free, it will be on purpose!! We must
choose to obey the Word of the Lord. That is **not**
bondage to the law, that is **freedom** in Christ!

Romans 5:21 tells us this: *"That as sin hath*
reigned unto death, even so might grace reign through
righteousness unto eternal life by Jesus Christ our
Lord." We all want to inherit the Kingdom of God.
We all want to walk in the promised blessings of the
Lord. We all want to be established in righteousness.

Romans 14:17 gives us yet another key to
getting the answers we need for this to be
accomplished in and through us: *"For the kingdom*

of God is not meat and drink; but righteousness, and peace, and joy in the Holy Ghost." Hear me, when I say we **must** establish ourselves in the righteousness of God, through Jesus Christ, and by the power of the Holy Ghost that is in us.

Get a plan, based on the Word of God, and then **activate** that plan. As the young people say today, "Just Do It." A good place to start is Psalm 112:1~4: *"Praise ye the Lord. Blessed is the man that feareth the Lord, that delighteth greatly in his commandments. His seed shall be mighty upon earth: the generation of the upright shall be blessed. Wealth and riches shall be in his house: and his righteousness endureth for ever. Unto the upright there ariseth light in the darkness: he is gracious, and full of compassion, and righteous."* So, what is the answer to our walking in blessing and righteousness? Fearing the Lord and delighting greatly in His commandments!

We need to understand something at this point in our teaching. Those that are not seeking after the righteousness of Christ for themselves, will not understand that in you. Do not expect the world or the religious to ever see your righteousness in Christ. Romans 10:3 says: *"For they being ignorant of God's*

116

righteousness, and going about to establish their own righteousness, have not submitted themselves unto the righteousness of God." They are just not willing to submit to and obey the Word of the Lord.

Several years ago, I had an experience that totally changed my way of thinking in some areas. I, like the Pharisees, thought that I had to be good enough, do enough, and accomplish enough, to really walk in holiness and righteousness. I had a desire in my heart to be all that I thought I could be because of the Word of God that was in my spirit. Then one day, the Lord decided to upset some more of my theology. I had been praying, what I thought was, diligently and seeking the Lord for guidance into a holier life. I told the Lord that I wanted to see His glory revealed. I truly desired to know what it would be like to walk in the realm of glory that I believed others have walked in. We were in a telethon at the television station, and I was scheduled to be on the air that night with Evangelist Mike Murdock. Of course, this called for a new outfit to wear (like he had seen everything I own! Ha!). I needed to go to the store to get a few things, so I started out with this in mind. I thought I would go to the grocery store first and then stop by the mall to find a new

117

dress. As I was driving to the store, the Spirit of the Lord spoke to my spirit to go to "Big Bear." I very seldom ever went to that store, simply because it was out of the way for me to do that; but, I just could not shake that strong impression for me to go to that particular store. It got so strong in my spirit that I really almost feared not going there. As I started in that direction, the Holy Spirit then spoke to my spirit again and said that He was going to manifest the glory of God to me in that store. Considering how I had been praying, I started to get excited at the thought that I would really see the glory of God.

I got to the store and as I went in, I tried to remember why I had even come. It was difficult for me to think about bread and milk at this point. As I went down one aisle, a little old man with a cane hanging on the handle of his grocery cart said, "Excuse me, miss, but can I ask you a question?" I said of course, and he proceeded to say, "Can you tell me anything about Rice-a-Roni?" Well, I kind of chuckled and told him the only thing I could tell him was that my husband did not like it. He thanked me and I walked on down the aisle.

I went on through the store looking for what I thought would be a manifestation of God's glory. I could not imagine what, in Big Bear, could be such as I was expecting. I went down the next aisle, and the Charmin toilet paper display had been knocked over. I proceeded to pick up the toilet paper and put it back on the display. I could not resist "squeezing the Charmin" as I replaced it on the shelf. I continued to look around for the glory that had been promised. The next thing I knew, this same little old man was again saying, "Excuse me, miss, but can I ask you another question?" I said sure and he asked me if I knew anything about Tuna Helper. I told him that my husband did like that.

He then told me that his wife had passed away just a few months before and that he had been eating in restaurants ever since. He was getting really tired of the food and thought he would try to cook something at home. The problem was he did not know how to cook and was looking for something quick, easy, and at the same time, tasty. I told him that he would probably like the Tuna Helper; so, he decided to get that and moved on.

I continued on my quest for the glory, trying to remember what I needed to buy, since my cart still did not have one item in it. I turned another corner and a woman said to me, "Excuse me, but can I ask you a question?" At this point I just burst out laughing and said, "Sure, why not. I haven't accomplished anything yet!" She then said, in a whisper and looking around as though fearful of being watched, "Are you a Christian?" Well that was certainly not what I was expecting to hear. I laughed and said, "Yes, I am." Looking around again, she then said, "A Spirit-filled Christian?" I whispered back to her, "Yes." She then proceeded to tell me that the Lord had spoken to her that morning to go to the Big Bear grocery store and He would reveal to her the meaning of walking in His glory. I thought to myself, "What is with God and the Big Bear store?"

She then told me an amazing story. She said she was walking around the store just looking at anything and everything, trying to get the understanding of what the Lord wanted her to see. He then spoke to her and told her to look at the door. She said she looked up and saw me walking in the door and there was a bright light over my head and the Lord told her to just follow that light. She said she watched me talk to the little old man about the Rice-a-Roni; she watched me pick up the Charmin toilet paper (I thought, "Oh no, she saw me squeeze the Charmin"); she then saw me talking again to the little old man about the Tuna Helper. She said the Lord then told her, "That's a manifestation of walking in the spirit with my glory being revealed." At this point the lady was shaking all over, and I was ready to burst into tears right there in the Big Bear store. She said she saw the love of God coming forth out of me as I just did what should be considered the "right" thing to do.

As I shared with her what the Lord had spoken to me on the way to the store, she was as amazed as I was. I then asked her if she had seen me before. I thought maybe she had seen me on television or at a gospel sing or perhaps my picture in the newspaper. She proceeded to break any bubble of pride I may have had rising up in me, and said, no, she had never seen me before in her life. She had no idea that I would be on television that very night with the world-famous Evangelist, Mike Murdock.

I trust you are picking up on the "tongue in cheek" terminology I am using here to get the point across. It had nothing to do with who I was; with who I might be acquainted; or with what I did as a profession. It all had to do with who He is in me and who I am in Him. I was so busy looking for the glory of the Lord to be revealed to me, that I missed just walking in it! The Lord is wanting to reveal His glory through us, not to us!

Do you get it? He wants us to get established in His righteousness . . . and He wants us to get the revelation of the fact that He, Jesus, is the "Way Maker."

Chapter 13

The Way Maker

I made reference to Isaiah 43:19 in a previous chapter concerning the new thing that the Lord said He would do. I want us to look at another portion of this scripture now in a different light. *"Behold, I will do a new thing; now it shall spring forth; shall ye not know it? I will even make a way in the wilderness, and rivers in the desert."*

He tells us that He will make a way in our wilderness. He will make a way where there seems to be no way! I believe the Lord wants His children to realize that He is the Way Maker. From the beginning of time, God the Father made the way of escape for us through that Lamb that was slain from the foundation of the world. (Revelation 13:8) Many times, we know that we have "eternal" life, but fail to realize that He provided life for us in the here and now. John 10:10 gives us this word of promise. *"The thief cometh not, but for to steal, and to kill, and to destroy: I am come that they might have life, and that they might have it more abundantly."* The Lord's desire for His children is that they walk in abundant life! I can just hear some of you saying in your heart now, "that's easy for you to say; you don't know what I'm going through." You are absolutely right. I do not know what you are going through, but I do know this; the Word of God says, He came to give us abundant life. If you are His child, then that promise belongs to you, but you have to take hold of it.

For years, I have ministered to born-again, spirit-filled believers that do not know how to walk in victory. They go from mountain top to valley; from victory to defeat; from being an overcomer to being overcome by the powers of the enemy. My heart cries out for them because they do not realize the price that Jesus paid for them to be the head and not the tail. (Deuteronomy 28:13) I hear the same cry from people time after time; "I can't get rid of this habit . . . I've tried." Well, you know the power of the Word of God. Allowing it to work in your life will bring victory.

Hebrews 12:1 gives us another word of instruction. *"Wherefore seeing we also are compassed about with so great a cloud of witnesses, let us lay aside every weight, and the sin which doth so easily beset us, and let us run with patience the race that is set before us."* This is making reference to the great "Hall of Faith" pioneers in Hebrews 11. The Lord, in essence, is telling us that there were those who went before us to help pave the way. They went through great battles of the flesh, yet came forth in victory. They had to die to their flesh, just like we do. If they could do it before Christ, how much more are we able to do it with the power of the blood and the authority of His name?

We can look at the lives of David, Moses, Elijah, Esther, Deborah, or any of the others that have walked down this road of life with the power of God's Word leading the way, and learn from their mistakes. David, a man after God's own heart, yet look at the mistakes he made. Does that mean we can do the same thing, knowing that God re-established David after he sinned? **No!** These recordings of past mistakes in the Word of God are **not** a license to sin, they are instructions to live by so we can **avoid** making the same mistakes.

I Corinthians 10:13 says: *"There hath no temptation taken you but such as is common to man: but God is faithful, who will not suffer you to be tempted above that ye are able; but will with the temptation also make a way to escape, that ye may be able to bear it."* The Lord is letting us know that there is nothing that can test or try us that He has not already made a way out for us; He is the Way Maker! Once we get this truth alive in our spirit man, and it becomes living Rhema word to us, we will begin to walk in that overcoming power that is rightfully ours as His child. Let's just look at a few of the Bible examples of the Lord being the Way Maker.

In Exodus, chapter three, we can find the story of Moses and the burning bush. We need to understand that the Lord did not just "plop" that bush down in front of Moses after he was on the mountain. I believe that bush was planted, watered, watched over, and protected by the hand of God for a long time before is was ever needed to speak to Moses.

God sent Elijah to the brook Cherith that He had laid out and prepared long before it was needed by Elijah. He had a group of birds, called ravens, being watched over and protected from harm, because they were going to be needed to feed the prophet. The widow woman's heart had already been prepared to feed the man of God. (I Kings 17:8~16)

Another account occurs in Jonah 1:17. *"Now the Lord had prepared a great fish to swallow up Jonah. And Jonah was in the belly of the fish three days and three nights."* In Matthew 17:27 we can read of provision being made in the New Testament. Jesus is speaking and He says: *"Notwithstanding, lest we should offend them, go thou to the sea, and cast an hook, and take up the first fish that cometh up; and when thou hast opened his mouth, thou shalt find a piece of money: that take, and give unto them for me and thee."* In order not to offend those that did not have the understanding of where they were walking, Jesus knew that He needed to conform to the ways of man and pay taxes. We are looking at the one who made the world, paying taxes on the very thing He helped create. Do you think for one moment that He could not have gotten out of that? Of course He could; but, there was a greater lesson in it for us if He once again could demonstrate how He really is the Way Maker. He created the fish; He created the coin that was in the fish's mouth; He even created the water for that fish to swim in. There was only one thing that He could not create . . . **Peter's obedience!** He made the way, but Peter had to obey.

In Luke 22:7~13 we can read another story of

the way being made. Jesus is getting ready to give His life on the cross for all mankind, but first He has to prepare the way. It is the time of the Passover and the Lord gives Peter and John their words of instruction. I am talking detailed instructions. I do not want to take the chance of you not reading this for yourself, so I am going to give you this entire portion of scripture: *"Then came the day of unleavened bread, when the passover must be killed. And He sent Peter and John, saying, 'Go and prepare us the passover, that we may eat.' And they said unto him, 'Where wilt thou that we prepare?' And he said unto them, 'Behold, when ye are entered into the city, there shall a man meet you, bearing a pitcher of water; follow him into the house where he entereth in. And ye shall say unto the goodman of the house, The Master saith unto thee, Where is the guestchamber, where I shall eat the passover with my disciples? And he shall show you a large upper room furnished: there make ready.' And they went, and found as he had said unto them: and they made ready the passover."* From the beginning of time, I believe Father God had a plan for this special night. Not only for the passover meal with the disciples, but with the man that had the upper room prepared.

He had already made the way. Of all the stories we could read about the Way Maker, my very favorite is found in Luke 19. I want you to get a mental image of the incident taking place here. If we can learn to visualize the Word of God, it will become a part of us in a real way. The story goes like this:

"And Jesus entered and passed through Jericho. And, behold, there was a man named Zacchaeus, which was the chief among the publicans, and he was rich. And he sought to see Jesus who he was; and could not for the press, because he was little of stature. And he ran before, and climbed up into a sycamore tree to see him: for he was to pass that way. And when Jesus came to the place, he looked up, and saw him, and said unto him, Zacchaeus, make haste, and come down; for today I must abide at thy house. And he made haste, and came down, and received him joyfully." (Luke 19:1~6)

Zacchaeus, a publican; hated by the Jews and Gentiles alike. He was a tax collector, and cheated people in order to become a rich man. Yet, something in him caused him to want to see who this Jesus was. The word tells us he was so short, he could not see over the crowd, so he ran and climbed a tree. This rich publican up a tree just to see this man called Jesus. When Jesus got to that place, He openly embarrassed and humiliated Zacchaeus. He looked up in the tree and called him by name and told him to get down out of that tree, for He was going to his house for dinner! I am sure that Zack was taunted about his short stature by those that hated him. Yet, here he was being called by name by this man Jesus. Do you suppose that he wondered how Jesus knew who he was? Do you suppose that he was worried about his dignity and position in life at this point in time? Now, here is the part of the story that I want you to get into your spirit. This is a "Lois" idea of what could have taken place many years before Zacchaeus was ever born.

God, the Father, calls two of His finest angels before His throne. He tells them that He has an important job for them to do. It is of utmost importance that they do not fail to accomplish this task. He then proceeds to give them instructions in planting a Sycamore tree just outside Jericho. He tells them the exact spot that He wants it to grow; He tells them to stand guard over it; make sure no camels step on it; make sure that the animals don't kill it off by eating the leaves. He tells them to be sure that it gets the water it needs to become a full-grown, healthy tree. I can just imagine the angels thinking to themselves; surely there is something more important than this that we could be doing! What they did not know was that, way down the road of life, there would be a little short man named Zacchaeus who would be so determined to see the promised son of God that he would lose his dignity; lay down his robes of self-righteousness; take off at a dead-heat run, to get to a place of position to be able to see the Lord.

The Father knew that he would need this tree to be a healthy, full-grown climber, that would become his way to the Son of God. The Lord knew he would be willing to press through the crowd and run ahead to get what he needed. Because of this, the way was made long before it was even needed. Can you hear what the Lord is saying to you? He has already made the way! He knew what we would need long before it was ever a reality in our life. He knew just where to plant the tree; to put the fish; to lay the brook; or to build that upper room that we would need to get to Him and to have our needs met.

He is our Way Maker!

Many of you may know of our weekly television program called "Firm Foundation." I want to give you a personal example of how the Lord became my Way Maker in getting me to move into His plan and purpose. The Lord had spoken to me several times about doing television; but, because I had worked in that arena for so many years I was well aware of the cost, not only in money, but in time and dedication as well. I was busy in ministry and did not really cherish the thought of another job to do. I had prayed about this many times, but was just so hesitant to step out in faith not knowing from where or how the finances could possibly come in. I could not figure out how "I" could get it done!

During this time, my heart started skipping beats; so much so that I had a difficult time feeling like I could breathe correctly. I finally went to the doctor and he put a monitor on me for 24 hours to see what it was really doing. They found out that my heart was missing way too many beats and put me in the hospital for tests. As I laid in that hospital bed, the Lord began to really speak to me about obedience. He has a way of getting my attention. Before it was over, I knew it was an "object lesson" for me, and I would come out of this experience with a greater knowledge of the power of God, if I listened and obeyed what I heard. After three days, they sent me home with no more answers than when I went in. My heart was still doing the same thing, just not nearly as much as it had been. The day after I came home, I called for an Intercessors meeting at my house.

We were in prayer and as I was praying about the direction of the ministry and the word of instructions concerning the television ministry, I said in my prayer, "Lord, you know my heart hesitates in stepping out in faith to do what I feel you have told me to do." I have taught for years that I believe that every manifestation of a physical problem in the flesh is rooted in a spiritual problem. The Lord then spoke to Mikki and told her to have me repeat what I had spoken. I spoke forth with the words of my mouth the very physical problem that was being manifested in me. My heart was hesitating over stepping out in faith to trust the Lord with the expenses of doing a weekly television production. My heart was skipping beats even as I spoke those words. Well, I have found a way to try the spirits that have been put in my path to see whether or not they be of God. I asked all of my intercessors to gather around me and lay hands on me and pray for me to lay down my own fears, insecurities, and controlling spirit and to enable me to have what I needed to completely trust Him with this new endeavor. The moment they finished praying my heart started beating normal and has done so ever since. That same day I began the process of getting prepared to do the television program. Within a matter of weeks the Lord had prepared the way; No! The way was already prepared; my obedience to His plan simply opened my eyes to be able to **see** the way. Week after week, He provided hundreds and hundreds of dollars for this work that I could never have imagined would come in. He wants us to understand:

He IS the Way Maker!

As He continues to make the way and as we continue to obey His word of instructions, we will become a part of that last day "turn aside generation" that will usher in the Kingdom of God.

Chapter 14

God's "Turn Aside" Generation

I was at a Leadership Conference at Morning Star Ministries, in North Carolina, when the Lord spoke to me concerning some things to come. I had gone back to the hotel and was going over some notes from one of the meetings when I heard the Lord say to my spirit: "I am raising up a 'turn aside generation' that will truly be movers and shakers in this last day." I really had no understanding of the impact this word would make on me. I received no more concerning this at the time, so I just put it on the shelf, as I have learned through experience to do.

Several weeks later, I was in prayer concerning a conference I was to speak at for the Women of Worth, in Birmingham, Alabama. The Holy Spirit then reminded me of that word I had heard in the hotel room in North Carolina. The name of the conference in Birmingham was: Movers, Shakers, and History Makers. I felt the Lord leading me into

His Word for a "word in season" for the Women of Worth, but also for the body of Christ.

Just what did the Lord mean when He spoke to me that He was going to raise up a "turn aside generation" that would truly be movers and shakers in this last day? I am going to look at two specific Bible examples of what it means to "turn aside;" and what will happen when we do that.

In Exodus 3:1~8, we can read the familiar story of Moses. Now, we all know that he was chosen by God from birth for a very special work of deliverance for God's chosen people. At this time in the story, he has fled from his call and is busy "doing his own thing." *"Now Moses kept the flock of Jethro his father in law, the priest of Midian: and he led the flock to the backside of the desert, and came to the mountain of God, even to Horeb. And the angel of the Lord appeared unto him in a flame of fire out of the midst of a bush: and he looked, and , behold, the bush burned with fire, and the bush was not consumed. And Moses said, I will now turn aside, and see this great sight, why the bush is not burnt. And when the Lord saw that he turned aside to see, God called unto him out of the midst of the bush, and said, Moses, Moses. And he said, Here am I. And he said, Draw not nigh hither: put off thy shoes from off thy feet, for the place whereon thou standest is holy ground. Moreover he said, I am the God of thy father, the God of Abraham, the God of Isaac, and the God of Jacob. And Moses hid his face; for he was afraid to look upon God. And the Lord said, I have surely seen the affliction of my people which are in Egypt, and have heard their cry by reason of their taskmasters; for I know their sorrows; And I am come down to deliver them out of the hand of the Egyptians, and to bring them up out of that land unto a good land and a large, unto a land flowing with milk and honey; unto the place of the Canaanites, and the Hittites, and the Amorites, and the Perizzites, and the Hivites, and the Jebusites."*

Now, in verse seven and eight, we have a "right now" applicable word from the Lord. You see, we all have struggles and trials and personal battles that we go through, and our needs are very real. Concerning these things, the Lord is saying to us, "I am come down to deliver." This speaks of direct intervention of the Lord concerning a specific need!

Hebrews 11:6 says: *"But without faith it is impossible to please him: for he that cometh to God must believe that he is and that he is a rewarder of them that diligently seek him."* We know what it means to "diligently" seek Him. The Lord spoke to me one day and told me that most of His children live with divided faith. We trust God for spiritual things, we trust money for financial security, and we trust people for our emotional needs to be met. But, the scripture that we just read says that He is a rewarder of those who diligently seek Him. This is a by-product of undivided faith. To those who earnestly seek and respond to His presence the Lord will reveal or manifest Himself in every area of our life. If we look to other people for our needs to be met we will be disappointed; man will fail us. If we look to ourselves we will be discouraged; we will never be able to get it all done. It is only when we look to God; we will be delivered. Moses is our example from which to learn.

Moses was raised in the palace of Pharaoh, yet he knew the call of God that was on his life. Therefore, when he saw an Israelite being afflicted by an Egyptian, he delivered him. It was almost as if he could not help himself. He thought his brothers would understand.

Acts 7:22~25 says: *"And Moses was learned in all the wisdom of the Egyptians, and was mighty in words and in deeds. And when he was full forty years old, it came to his heart to visit his brethren the children of Israel. And seeing one of them suffer wrong, he defended him, and avenged him that was oppressed, and smote the Egyptian: For he supposed his brethren would have understood how that God by his hand would deliver them: but they understood not."* First of all, note that it says, *"and when he was full forty years old . . ."* when the fullness of time had come. In God's timing; when it was the right time. God's timetable and our timetable is not usually the same thing. It is not usually even in the same year; let alone month or day!

Well, as a result of this entire episode with the Egyptian, Moses fled into the wilderness. There are those in the church today who are perplexed, feeling that others should accept and make room for their calling. But it is still true today; the brethren do not understand. Our dependence must abide in God alone! Moses fled into the wilderness where he kept the flock of his father-in-law, Jethro. He was not functioning in his calling, but he was not discouraged or bitter. He was still leading sheep toward the mountain of God (first the natural, then the spiritual). He was in the "comfort zone" of God's

139

permissive will. We need to notice that the Lord did not speak to Moses until after he had turned aside to see (verse 4). I believe the Lord was just waiting for Moses to notice and respond to His manifested presence.

That burning bush may have been there for years; but, Moses was so intent on "moving toward the mountain of God" that it remained unseen. Finally, his self ability became so depleted that he noticed and was willing to turn aside. The bush burned, but was not consumed. That tells me that that bush is still burning today! The Lord's presence is still being manifested through intervention. There is a progression in our Christian experience which, if followed, will lead us to that place of being willing to turn aside to see His manifest presence.

I love to correlate the Old and New Testament. In Revelation 1:10~15, we can see a similar account of the impact of "turning aside." *"I was in the Spirit on the Lord's day, and heard behind me a great voice, as of a trumpet, Saying, I am Alpha and Omega, the first and the last: and , What thou seest, write in a book, and send it unto the seven churches which are in Asia; unto Ephesus, and unto Smyrna, and unto Pergamos, and unto Thyatira, and unto Sardis, and unto Philadelphia, and unto Laodicea. And I turned to see the voice that spake with me. And being turned, I saw seven golden candlesticks; And in the midst of the seven candlesticks one like unto the Son of man, clothed with a garment down to the foot, and girt about with paps with a golden girdle. His head and his hairs were white like wool, as white as snow; and his eyes were as a flame of fire; And his feet like unto fine brass, as if they burned in a furnace; and his voice as the sound of many waters."*

When John heard the voice, he chose to "turn aside" to see! When he did, he saw the manifested presence of the Lord. The "burning bush" in another form. His eyes were as a flame of fire!! The Lord wants us to come to the end of our own strengths and abilities and acknowledge Him! Only then will He respond with a revelation of His manifested presence. Only when we "turn aside" will we be able to see. When Moses turned, the Lord said, "Do not come near here, put off your sandals from your feet; for the place on which you stand is holy ground." (Exodus 3:5)

The Lord was saying to him, "You have walked in the shoes of the world long enough. You have turned aside to see My presence, and you are now in a new walk. Your feet are in a holy place. I Am that I AM, is now leading and directing your steps in a new direction." When John turned aside he saw the manifestation of the Son of God; that bush that burned. When he did, he fell at His feet as though dead. He was on holy ground.

I looked through some church history to see the movers and shakers of days gone by. I stand in awe of the power of God that was manifested through them. I am talking about people like Kathryn Kulman, Aimee Simple McPherson, A. A. Allen, Smith Wigglesworth, or William Branham. One thing they all had in common; they all had to be willing to do something they had never done before. They all had to step out in faith and just trust God in a way they never had before; they all had to be willing to "turn aside" to see the manifested presence and glory of God.

So many today have been like Moses; rejected by their brothers. Because of that they have run to another "mountain of God" to try to replace the call of God on their life with a temporary "good work." You will never see the glory of God if you are not consumed by Him. Hebrews 12:29 tells us that our God is a "consuming fire."

I looked up the words: mover, shaker, and history maker. I found this to be very interesting.

Mover: The person or thing that gives motion or impels to action.

Shaker: A person or thing that shakes or agitates; as the shaker of the earth.

History Makers: According to Webster's "1828" Dictionary; history and story, are the same word differently written. We can, as Christians, conclude that history is actually; "His story." Maker, is one that makes, forms, shapes, or molds . . . or the creator.

You can choose to be a mover, one that impels others to action; a shaker, one that agitates or shakes things up; or you can make a decision to be a His-story maker, one that will be a part of the last day revival that will help make, form, shape, and mold others into His likeness and after His image!

Margaret Browning said, "Every bush is aflame with the fire of God, but only those who see, take off their shoes. The rest just pick the berries."

I decided a long time ago, that I do not want to just be a berry picker. The Lord is looking for a people that will be willing to "turn aside;" and when they do, they will receive a fresh revelation of who He is!

It's Time!

Romans 8:19 says: *"For the earnest expectation of the creature waiteth for the manifestation of the sons of God."* The world is just waiting to see a manifestation of the glory of God. For this to happen, there **must be** a people that will be willing to make Him "Lord of All."

Chapter 15

Lord Of All

We are given an account of what it truly means to make Jesus "Lord of all" in Luke 6:46~49: *"And why call ye me, Lord, Lord, and do not the things which I say? Whosoever cometh to me, and heareth my sayings, and doeth them, I will show you to whom he is like: He is like a man which built an house, and digged deep, and laid the foundation on a rock: and when the flood arose, the stream beat vehemently upon that house, and could not shake it: for it was founded upon a rock. But he that heareth, and doeth not, is like a man that without a foundation built an house upon the earth; against which the stream did beat vehemently, and immediately it fell; and the ruin of that house was great."* I want us to take note here that the Lord said, "when the flood arose," not if . . . it is a settled issue; we will have floods come into our life, but if our house is built upon the Rock of Jesus Christ, it will not be shaken. Once the issue of

Lordship is settled, then other matters of life will be settled. There are several points I want to make here that, once they come to life in our spirit, will change our life.

1. Lordship will settle the issue or question of "position" in your life. Who are you? Romans 8:14 tells us: *"For as many as are led by the Spirit of God, they are the sons of God."*

2. With that comes a settling of the "permission" issue in your life. When Jesus becomes Lord, you come into a place of responsibility and accountability. I Corinthians 6:19~20 says: *"What? know ye not that your body is the temple of the Holy Ghost which is in you, which ye have of God, and ye are not your own? For ye are bought with a price: therefore glorify God in your body, and in your spirit, which are God's."*

3. Lordship will settle the "profession" issue. You will live what you profess when Jesus is Lord of your life. Malachi 2:6 says: *"The law of truth was in his mouth, and iniquity was not found in his lips: he walked with me in peace and equity* (justly, or in right standing), *and did turn many away from iniquity." "Herein is my Father glorified, that ye bear much fruit; so shall ye be my disciples."* (John 15:8)

"If ye love me, keep my commandments." (John 14:15) *"If ye keep my commandments, ye shall abide in my love; even as I have kept my Father's commandments, and abide in His Love."* (John 15:10) Now look at verse 11: *"These things have I spoken unto you, that my joy might remain in you, and that your joy might be full."* The only way we can have the joy of the Lord remain, dwell, or stay within us, is to allow Him to be Lord of All. Our promise that goes with this is fullness of joy in our life!

This is part of settling the "profession" issue. If the world sees your joy, your words of profession will be needed much less. The world cannot hear what we are saying because of what they are seeing. It is difficult to tell the difference between the world and the church. The Lord is saying to us, "This ought not be so." We are to be doers of the Word, and not hearers only. (James 1:22)

4. Lordship will settle the "possession" issue. Who owns the things in your life? In Mark, the tenth chapter, we have the story of the rich, young ruler being tested. He seemingly wanted to follow the Lord but just could not let go of the worldly possessions. Had he only realized the Lord would have given him much more than he had if he had only been willing to let go of what was in his hand. It is not what you have, but, what has you. Jesus gave the answer in verse 24b: *". . .how hard is it for them that trust in riches to enter into the kingdom of God!"*

Only when you completely dedicate and consecrate your life to the Lord, and make Him Lord of All, will you walk in victory. It will not matter what storms rage in your life; it will not matter what the world's systems may do; it will not matter what man may say; you will be an overcomer!

And I say: **It's Time!**

The Lord gave me a poem several years ago that I want to share with you. It was at a time in my life when I was truly learning what it really means to make Him Lord of All. I was having to go through a valley of despair and loneliness in order to find out that I could not do it myself.

My Name's "I AM"

There was a time in my life
I tried to walk alone
Without my Heavenly Father
To show the way toward home

Lord Of All

I can do this thing called life
What's all the fuss about?
I had no thoughts of days to come
They were mine, I had no doubt

But, as I traveled down the road
Life's trials came my way
I realized there must be more
Than just another day

I tried to fall back on the God
Heard of from childhood days
He wasn't there, what could be wrong?
"I WAS" was not His name

I seemed to yearn for things unseen
Someday, God's Love will come to me
But, in my heart, I heard Him say
"My Name is not, 'I WILL BE' "

I am a God of Everyday
A God of Peace and Grace
If you will only let Me in
My Love will fill that place

I have so long awaited
For you to take My Hand
And realize, I'm a "RIGHT NOW GOD"
You see, My Name's "I AM"

I want my life to be so consumed with the presence of God that people's lives will be radically changed from just being around me. I really do think "It's Time." How about you? If we allow the Lord to do in us what He desires to do then our lives **will** Make A Difference!

Chapter 16

Lord, Let Me Make A Difference

Matthew 5:14~16 gives us the word of instruction we need to make a difference in the world we live in. *"Ye are the light of the world. A city that is set on a hill cannot be hid. Neither do men light a candle, and put it under a bushel, but on a candlestick; and it giveth light unto all that are in the house. Let your light so shine before men, that they may see your good works, and glorify your Father which is in heaven."* Let your light so shine before men that they may see your good works, and glorify God! This tells me that the Lord intends for us to allow our works to be seen.

Years ago, I sang a song at my Grandpa Green's church. The name of it was, "Ashamed." I do not know who wrote it, but the message was powerful. It talked about being so busy getting everything done that needed to be done that the Lord was left out. The words to the chorus went like this:

Ashamed, Ashamed, I felt Ashamed
I hadn't done one thing for my Lord
What would I do, What could I say
If He came back today
I'm ashamed, forgive me, please Lord

Many times, I have had to ask myself that question: "Would I stand ashamed before Him, if He came back today?" My heart cries out to the Lord to just do with me whatever is needed to get me where I need to be in Him.

I had an experience, several years ago, that forever changed my life. As I share this, I trust the Lord will speak to your heart, and you, too, will cry out to Him to change your heart and make you into His image and after His likeness.

Our gospel group was scheduled to sing at a church in Columbus, Ohio. We had never been to this church before, but we knew the pastor from working at the television station. We arrived at the church, which was located right on Main Street in downtown Columbus. We were the only white folk there. Now, that has never been a problem for me, but we got the impression that the people were definitely expecting something different from us, considering the name of our group was:

"The Soul Seekers"

We were warmly received as we started to minister with our Southern Gospel style music. The part of town where we were located had all kinds of occult shops, bars, drugs, and prostitutes readily available. As we were singing, a young man approximately thirty years old, came stumbling into the church. He stood at the door, leaned over, and just looked at me up front singing. He kind of shook his head, turned around, and went back outside. It was not very long, until he was back again. This continued throughout the service. He would stumble in, shake his head, and stumble back out again. It was obvious that he was either drunk or high on something. After this happened several times, I stopped right in the middle of a song and began to pray. I prayed for the Lord to just wrap His arms of love around this young man and let him know how much He loved him, right where he was.

At the end of the service, I gave an altar call, and again this young man was standing at the back of the church just shaking his head as he turned and went back out the door. After the service ended, I was at the back of the church at the record table with the others in the group. We needed more tapes and records brought in off the bus, so I stepped out the door to go get them. Just as I stepped outside, this tall, young man that had been coming in and out all evening stepped around the corner of the church porch and grabbed my arm. He leaned down in my face, and I could not help but marvel at the whites of his eyes. There **were** no whites! They were so blood shot, there was nothing but red and blue and yellow lines all throughout his eyes.

He was holding very tightly to my arm and was right in my face. He then said to me, "Lady, can I ask you a question?" Well, I must admit, I was really wondering what was going to take place at this point in time. I had been doing a study on "Angels" and had been reading Dr. Billy Graham's book, "Angels, Angels, Angels," and Pastor Roland Buck's book, "Angels On Assignment." So, my first thought was, "Oh Lord, where are my angels when I need them?" But, I proceeded to answer him with, "You can ask me anything you like." He then proceeded to say in a very slurred voice, "Lady, how long you been doin' this, this, this. . ." I said to him, "Doing what?" He then said, "all this preachin', singin', and every-thing." I simply said, "Oh, a long time." He then said,

"I want to tell you something lady, I've been on the street since I was twelve years old. I've been a pimp, and I've been a pusher. I'm hooked on drugs, and I'm an alcoholic, and **nobody** gives a damn! Are you going to tell me that your Jesus cares about me?"

Well, it didn't take long for the Holy Ghost to take over. Remember what I prayed in the middle of the church service: that the Lord would just wrap His arms of love around this young man and let him know how much God cared for him. I reached up and took hold of his other hand and said, "I sure am going to tell you that **my Jesus cares about you**. He knows where you have been, he knows where you are, but most of all, He knows where He wants you to go." Well, when I took hold of his hand, he let go of my arm, so I grabbed the other hand. I then said, "Can I pray for you?" He was so shook up that I had taken hold of him, that he couldn't seem to answer. So, I didn't wait for him to decide against prayer. I just started praying. I said, "Oh, Lord, wrap Your arms of love around this young man and let him know that You died for him, that You gave Your life so he could be set free. Touch him now Lord, and set him free! In Jesus Name, Amen!" When I looked up at him, he was standing ram-rod straight staring at me with eyes as big as saucers like I was the one with the problem! The most amazing thing was that his eyes were as clear as mine! Hallelujah!! The Lord had touched this young man in a way that I cannot even fathom.

About that time, Pastor John stepped outside the church. He was excited, to say the least, shouting, "Oh, Sister Lois, are you all right?" You see he didn't know **who** had who! I told him what had happened. He found out that this young man had not had anything to eat for three days. He had lived in Columbus, Ohio, all his life, and no one had ever told him that Jesus loved him. The pastor found him a room to stay in; saw to it that he was fed; and proceeded to let him know what had happened when I prayed for him. He was stone-cold sober immediately! Now that is the power of the Holy Ghost!!

Has the church failed, or what? Right in downtown Columbus, Ohio, and no one had ever witnessed to him about the love of Jesus! Well, that night when we got home, it was late and I was exhausted, but I just could not go to sleep. I went out to the kitchen table and sat there with my Bible open. About three o'clock in the morning, as I sat there thinking about that young man's life, the Lord spoke to my heart and said these words to me that forever changed my life. He said, "What if you had not been willing to be the only white people in an all black church, in the bad part of town? If you will only be willing and obedient, I will use you to forever make a difference in the lives of multitudes of people. You will someday see this young man on the streets of heaven, just because you allowed Me to work through you." Well, needless to say, by this time I was a broken, bawling mess. The Lord then took me to Matthew 5:16 that again says: *"Let your light so shine before men, that they may see your good works, and glorify your Father which is in heaven."*

That night I wrote the song, "Lord, Let Me Make A Difference." Hear the words and apply them to your life:

There's a world that's sick and dying
They don't know which way to go
And all the while we've had the answer
Now It's time we let them know
Help me be a willing vessel, Lord
You're the potter, I'm the clay
And let me make a difference
In someone's life today

It's Time

Lord, let me make a difference
In someone's life today
As they wonder in the darkness
Let my light help show the way
Let my hands reach out to help my brother
Share Your love with one another
And let me make a difference
In someone's life today

Since the day that I met Jesus
Life has never been the same
Even though I still have problems
I can call upon His name
My strength shall be my joy in Him
I'll let it shine before all men
Then I can make a difference
In someone's life today

Lord, let me make a difference
In someone's life today
As they wonder in the darkness
Let my light help show the way
Let my hands reach out to help my brother
Share Your love with one another
And let me make a difference in someone's life today.

If I go by way of the grave before the Lord's return and I have anything said about me at my eulogy, I want it to be said:

"She Made A Difference"

My hope and my heart's desire for this book is that all who read it will put their own name in all of these experiences that I have written about. That the body of Christ will have a God given revelation that it really **is time** for the church to rise up in the power of His might and become what He says we already are.

Epilogue

Every year, for many years now, the Lord has given me a word for the new year coming in. He usually gives this to me when I am fasting and praying at the end of the year. This past year, as I was getting ready for our January Conference, I had not yet heard a word for the New Year. It was January 12th, and I just thought maybe the Lord was changing the way He had always done things.

As I sat in my hotel room, praying about the conference, the Lord began to speak to my spirit. It came so quickly that I could hardly keep up with writing down what I was hearing. At first, I thought the Lord was giving me a word for the conference itself. As I finished writing down what I had received, I realized that this was a word for the body of Christ.

I also believe that it is a VITAL word that must be received and obeyed. I ask that you hear with ears of the spirit, what the Spirit is saying to the Church.

January 12, 2001

As I sat in my hotel room, seeking the Lord in prayer for His perfect will to be accomplished at my next day's conference, I heard His voice speak to me the following words:

"It's time for God to arise and His enemies be scattered." I knew this scripture, so I opened my Bible to Psalm 68 and read the following: *"Let God arise, let his enemies be scattered: let them also that hate him flee before him. As smoke is driven away, so drive them away: as wax melteth before the fire, so let the wicked perish at the presence of God. But let the righteous be glad; let them rejoice before God: yea, let them exceedingly rejoice."* (Psalm 68:1~3)

Since I was seeking the Lord in behalf of my up-coming meeting, I naturally thought He was speaking to me concerning that. I then heard Him again speak to my spirit the following: "Did I not warn My people of the consequences of calling black white; and white black? Did I not warn of calling good evil; and evil good?" I turned to Isaiah 5:20 to read: *"Woe unto them that call evil good, and good evil; that put darkness for light, and light for darkness; that put bitter for sweet, and sweet for bitter."*

I then heard the following prophetic words coming forth from the Holy Ghost: "There is and has been, a generation in the church that have stiffened their necks and turned away their hearts from My Truth. The Day of Reckoning is at hand. I am about to arise; and all shall see My enemies scattered by My hand, saith the Lord. My true church will arise with power and authority, and My glory shall be seen by all! As My children of obedience begin to walk in the fullness of My manifest presence in their lives, I will raise My scepter to them and they shall know I am well pleased. As they continue in My love; as My name is lifted up and glorified; and as the strength and power of My might comes forth in them, the fulfillment of My Word shall be seen. The truth came first to My chosen people, through the covenant with My servant, Abraham. It was then, by My design, given unto the Gentiles. Do you not understand that I would that all men be saved: and yet many continue to turn away from My grace and love. The Day of Reckoning is upon you, saith the Lord.

Many that have stood, even in the pulpit, and declared My name, have but gall in their bellies and bitterness in their hearts. Because of their rejection of My healing and forgiveness, they will soon feel the rejection of My Spirit. They have chosen to walk over the line into the enemy's camp. They have made the choice to declare, by their own actions, that they are the enemy of the Lord. Many have been overtaken by greed and lust of the flesh, and continue to say, "thus saith the Lord." Did I not give warning to them that call black white; and white black? Did I not warn against calling good evil; and evil good?

It's Time For The Lord To Arise, And His Enemies Be Scattered!

I am putting forth a call to repentance, saith the Lord. I am sending My servants; My messengers; and My prophets, across the land to declare the day of the Lord. I am causing the shofar to sound declaring unto all that will hear, "The Day Of The Lord Is At Hand!"

You say, "You want to see My face;" You say, "You want to know My ways;" You say, "You want to give your all;" You say, "You are willing to obey." And yet, the smallest word of instruction that is VITAL to your well-being, is pushed aside and ignored. Did I not say, Forgive, and you shall be forgiven? Did I not warn against fulfilling the lusts of the flesh? Did I not speak forth time and time again: "Worship Me; for I desire a people to worship with a pure heart."

Many have come into My courtyard with the filth of the world clinging to their garments, and, for a season, I allowed My servants to wipe away the dirt. But, the season is changing. All will give account for their own actions. Many of My priests have fallen and failed; but NO MORE will that be a way of blame or escape for My children of disobedience. YOU WILL GIVE ACCOUNT!

I have provided all you need to abound in My grace. I have given My very best to remove your very worst. And yet, so many refuse to come.

CHANGE! CHANGE!! CHANGE!!! Hear the winds of change blowing upon My Church; My Body; My Bride. I WILL HAVE a body that is rightly fitted together! I WILL HAVE a beautiful bride that IS prepared. I WILL HAVE a people that desire to be in My presence; and I will make Myself known unto them, saith the Lord. This is the day of the return of the stolen property of My children! This is the time of retrieving back that which the enemy has stolen. He has stolen your HEALTH; he has stolen your WEALTH; he has stolen your PEACE; he has stolen your SHEEP; he has stolen your HOPE; he has stolen your BLESSING; he has stolen your FAMILY; he has stolen your INHERITANCE; but, I say to My children of OBEDIENCE. "This is the time and day of the restoration of ALL THINGS.

GET READY..........GET READY.........GET READY.....

To go forth in the power of My might," saith the Lord; "and you WILL BE VICTORIOUS IN ALL YOUR WAYS," THUS SAITH THE LORD!

I believe I, along with many others around the world, have heard basically, the same word from the Lord. A word of WARNING; a word of CORRECTION; a word of CHASTISEMENT; a word of ENCOURAGEMENT; but most of all a word of PROMISE to His children of obedience in this NEW MILLENNIUM.

IT'S TIME......Let's prepare our hearts for the revelation of God's manifest presence and glory on this earth.

LAH/SSEA

Afterword

The "Firm Foundation" that my personal relationship and ministry has stood on for over twenty-five years has been Proverbs 3:5~6: *"Trust in the Lord with all thine heart; and lean not unto thine own understanding. In all thy ways acknowledge him, and he shall direct thy paths."*

He has done JUST THAT ! As I close out this, another chapter in my own life, I want to repeat something that I spoke in the closing portion of my last book, "The Bride Wears Combat Boots." It is a quote from Pastor Kelly Varner's book, "Whose Right It Is," and it certainly bears repeating. He said, "All spiritual warfare must be waged from the posture of Jesus' finished work. Our Lord rests within the rent veil, the enthroned ruler over all enemies. Unless we stand and fight from the perspective of solid resurrection ground, we will continue to do no more than cover ourselves with sweat and beat the air."

Jesus said, "It Is Finished" as He gave up His life for you and me. "It's Time" we realize, He said what He meant, and He meant what He said.........IT IS FINISHED! THAT'S the perspective of SOLID RESURRECTION GROUND.

Other Titles Available:

The Bride Wears Combat Boots - $10.00

Other Products Also Available:

2 TAPE SERIES: $12.00 EACH SET

A Revelation Of God's Glory
Beauty For Ashes
Eagle Saints Arise
Expectant Faith And The Suddenlys Of God
Fan In The Hand Of God
Free To Be
January Jubilee - The Best Is Yet To Come!
January Jubilee - Release, Restore, Refresh
Kings And Priests Unto The Lord
Life In The Spirit
Once Upon A Time
Praise, Worship, And Intercession
The Bride Wears Combat Boots

3 TAPE SERIES: $17.00 EACH SET

Apple Of God's Eye
Come, Let Us Go To The Mountain Of God
Foundations For Prophetic Ministry
Going Behind The Veil
Going For The Gold

ALL PRICES **INCLUDE** SHIPPING AND HANDLING!

To Schedule Lois A. Hoshor or the
Soul Seekers for a Gospel Sing,
Revival, Conference, or Speaking
Engagement, call or write to the
address below.

Lois A. Hoshor
Soul Seekers Evangelistic Association
PO Box 547
Thornville, OH 43076-0547
Ph: (740) 246-6272
Fax: (740) 246-6694
E-Mail: soulseekers7@itilink.com